Cases in Managerial Finance

M. J. Murray

Winona State University

KOLB Kolb Publishing Company   Boulder, Colorado

Printed in the United States of America.

Library of Congress Catalog Card Number 94–75889

ISBN: 1–878975–43–9

Kolb Publishing Company
6395 Gunpark Drive, Suite N, Boulder, CO 80301
(303) 530-7778   FAX (303) 530-7773

Introduction

For most students, their first case study class is a little unsettling. Case studies involve great uncertainty, are time–consuming, and, initially, produce little tangible gain. But with practice, organization, and commitment to the process, students truly become problem solvers and begin to "see" how they will use the knowledge they have accumulated through their studies. Looking back, many students identify their case study class as one of the more important experiences in their educational development.

Cases are a good vehicle to teach a course in advanced Corporate Finance because the format also teaches problem–solving skills. And because case study generally involves a write–up, the format develops writing and presentation skills—truly life–long skills. Thus, while some Finance topics must be sacrificed with this approach, given the time available in a course, the ability to solve significant, sometimes quite complex, business finance problems is a tangible outcome of the case study method.

Process of Case Study

If the cases are indeed challenging, they are best solved by a group of students, usually three to four. No matter how intelligent, analytical, and creative one individual may be, that student still represents only one perspective. Additional students bring additional perspectives as well as the basis for discussion and argument over various facets of the case. The time–consuming nature of case analysis and presentation demands a sharing of the load. Organization skills are generally quite poor at first but develop rapidly through the term with the various trials and tribulations of group work. The product of a well–functioning group is always superior to that of the brightest of individuals. And students will soon discover in their careers that group work is how business gets done.

The specific process usually involves each member of the group reading the case, thinking about the issues it raises, doing their own analyses, and then meeting with the other group members to discuss the case. If each member is prepared, this meeting time is usually enjoyable and productive. From this, each individual member assumes some responsibility for a part of the case and then, with one or more subsequent meetings, the individual parts are assembled into an integrated whole. Students naturally stop to admire their work, take a breath, but then must begin again on the next case. It can be a little grueling at times.

In order to channel energies into the case itself, then, a uniform report format is highly recommended. In this way students need not waste time thinking about the format and can concentrate on how to make their points more effectively, and more persuasively.

A Suggested Report Format

Although some may argue that all business reports should begin with an "Executive Summary," my experience has been that "executives" study such reports far too little, and giving them an executive summary lets them off the hook too easily. Besides, well–written reports should be succinct, well–organized summaries in the first place, and "executives" should be able to glean relevant points and information from them with ease.

The first section, then, would be the BACKGROUND. It should include a little about the nature of the business, a description of its current situation, and in particular, its current financial condition. It should be brief but describe the situation adequately for someone who is not familiar with the case. It should always be written last, because the distilling process of what information is germane, and what is not, cannot be known until the end.

The second section should be the STATEMENT OF THE PROBLEM. Students initially tend to focus on the symptoms, not the underlying problem(s). It should also give a sense of what related problems might be, and the extent of the problem. How serious is it? In what way? This statement should be one paragraph—a maximum of two or three sentences.

The next section, ANALYSIS OF ALTERNATIVES, should contain the meat of the report. What are the alternatives? Students and business managers often tend to dismiss some alternatives out of hand, perhaps because they don't want to choose them or because they don't seem to make much sense at first. The advantages and disadvantages of each alternative should be clearly identified, and the actual (hard) analysis of each should be provided. The discussion of alternatives is often biased, suggesting the choice came before an objective analysis was conducted.

From these analyses, a SOLUTION should be chosen and supported. Why is this solution the best one? How will it be implemented? How will progress be monitored and success be determined? While more than one answer may be possible, some are better than others, and it is up to the student to convince the reader that his or her solution is the "right" one.

Nature of These Cases

Cases come in all shapes and sizes, across most disciplines. At one extreme, they represent little more than an extended problem set. As such, they are simple, straightforward applications of concepts and formulae which produce single right answers. At the other end, they are highly unstructured, specific company, specific problem situations which accommodate a wide range of "solutions."

The cases here represent something in between—in many ways possessing the strengths of each extreme without the attendant weaknesses. In particular, these cases are based on real companies and real problems, accommodate more than one "right" answer, but are directed so as to lead students through the specific applications of Finance theory (including formulae), necessary to provide the information base on which to develop a solution. Their length and complexity are also something in between. A distinguishing feature of these cases is that they are integrative in nature, thereby allowing the student to see how a proposed solution to a particular problem affects other facets of the firm's financial condition.

The types of problems can be seen in the Contents. The industries are listed on the next page, by SIC code. As can be seen, there is great diversity and a good balance between traditional goods–producing industries and increasingly important service–producing activities.

Goods–Producing		Service–Producing	
232	Men's & Boys' Clothing	401	Railroads
245	Wood Buildings	491	Electric Services
262	Paper Mills	514	Groceries, Wholesale
273	Book Publishers	541	Grocery Stores
281	Industrial Chemicals	596	Nonstore Retailers
331	Blast Furnaces & Steel	655	Subdividers & Developers
354	Metalworking Machinery	679	Misc. Investing
356	Industrial Equipment	701	Hotels, Motels
369	Misc. Electrical Equipment	737	Computer Services
379	Misc. Transportation Equipment	871	Construction Services

Case Abstracts

Finally, specific case abstracts are provided here to give students and instructors alike a sense of what issues are involved in each selection. I have found it useful to reproduce these in my syllabus for the cases I choose for the term because it gives students some idea of what they will be learning in the course, much like a course outline in a traditional class.

Servais Stores, Inc.

Due to rapid expansion and an increasingly intensive competitive environment, Servais Stores, a major operator and franchiser of convenience stores, finds itself on the brink of bankruptcy. In order to assess the company's alternatives properly, a thorough analysis of the firm's condition is necessary, as is a forecast of its plan(s) to address the problem.

Ohio, Indiana and Central States Corporation

Ohio, Indiana and Central States Corporation is the parent company of a rejuvenated regional railroad which feels threatened by the current period of consolidation in the industry. In order to remain independent, the company must critically analyze its operations and finances in terms of industry norms, and choose those courses of action which will lead to high market valuations and thus make it a less attractive target.

Manchester Inns, Inc.

Manchester Inns is the owner and manager of some 200 motor inns in the U.S., but it has been stagnant for the past several years. The company feels locked into its current situation and needs to take some dramatic action to break out. In order to strengthen its financial position and take advantage of opportunities in its industry, one plan involves liquidating some assets and refunding long–term debt, but it is not altogether clear how this can be achieved.

Riordan Industries, Inc.

A diversified commercial and industrial equipment manufacturer, Riordan Industries has struggled to rebound from the recession and now feels that it can further its progress with the expansion of industrial and analytical instruments lines. With only limited success itself, the company believes that a joint venture with an existing instruments firm, leading ultimately to a merger of their operations, would be the best approach to achieving this objective. In the process, it hopes to reduce its variability in sales, earnings, cash flows, and returns.

Fystrom Chemical Company, Inc.

Fystrom Chemical Company is a rapidly growing specialty chemical producer who is considering a major plant expansion into Mexico, as an alternative to the modification of an existing facility in the U.S. This decision requires a thorough analysis of the cash flows associated with each choice and the application of the proper economic concepts and tax law which produce those cash flows. Non–quantifiable issues, which are always a part of such decisions, must be confronted here as well.

Mosher Pumps, Inc.

Mosher Pumps, a medium–sized producer of industrial high pressure pumps, is considering a major expansion into a new product line of painting equipment and accessories, engineered and marketed specifically for retail customers. Because of the scope of this project and the uncertainty of a new market, the company wants to quantify thoroughly the risks involved.

Tenneson Property Investors, Inc.

A real estate investment trust, Tenneson Property Investors, Inc., is considering two possible investments in apartment properties that have possible alternative and additional uses in the future. Given that these uses are uncertain, as are the cash flows that they would generate if they did materialize, the question facing the trust is how, specifically, they can factor these future possibilities into their decision today to invest. If the apartment investments themselves were sufficiently profitable and met all other investment objectives, the decision would be easy. But, alas, life is rarely so simple.

Mobile Energy, Inc.

Cost of capital is an abstract or "academic" issue to many finance practitioners. In fact it has real dollar impact if not properly measured and applied in capital investment decisions. This case with Mobile Energy, a diversified electric utility, provides ample opportunity to explore the wide range of issues associated with the cost of capital concept, and its application.

Northern Woods Campers, Inc.

A camper manufacturer, Northern Woods Campers, Inc., is considering a major investment in a cabinetry facility, but it has no idea what a minimum acceptable return should be. The effort to estimate its cost of capital is complicated first by the fact that virtually all long–term funds in this industry are equity capital. Second, the common stock of this company, while public, is not actively traded. And third, the highly cyclical and volatile sales and earnings performance of many of this industry's participants makes it difficult even to use comparison data for an estimate. The difficulty/uncertainty of this task, however, makes it no less needed.

O'Malley Steel, Inc.

O'Malley Steel is a minimill steel producer who has decided to commit to a major expansion of its production capacity. The company has been very conservative in its financial policy because of the tenuous nature of the industry and the markets it serves. It must now consider carefully the risks and rewards of leverage in its current effort to expand.

Boyesen Industries, Inc.

In spite of a successful record of growth and profitability in the textile mill products and apparel industries over many years, Boyesen Industries finds itself with an important segment of its stockholders unhappy with its current dividend policy. A major question that must be answered is whether a more generous payout can be sustained.

Johanek Corporation

In an effort to expand, complement its existing activities, and moderate the swings in revenues and earnings, Johanek Corporation (a large, regional residential and commercial builder), is interested in developing its fledgling financial services business. But in order to do so, it must add significantly to its computer capabilities. The company must choose between two competing systems and among a variety of financing methods.

Dahlberg's, Inc.

A large food wholesaler is considering an acquisition. While the basic task is to develop valuation estimates, the projection of appropriate cash flows and a cost of capital estimate are integral parts of the analysis. And since this does represent a relatively large acquisition, the financing mix is an important aspect of both the cash flow projection and the cost of capital calculation. Other nonfinancial issues need to be included as well, and thus, it is a fairly comprehensive case.

Potawatomi Paper Company

An investment banking firm flush with cash is planning to acquire an attractive though struggling paper company, Potawatomi Paper, and take it private. It hopes to manage a turnaround and then capitalize on its efforts through a later public offering. The particular circumstances here offer a unique opportunity to consider the full range of possible debt/equity combinations in financing this acquisition.

Cognoscere Corporation

Cognoscere Corporation, a software developer with a strong presence in the midrange computer market segment, is actively seeking acquisitions. An agreement in principle has been reached with a very successful niche player in the same industry, but they cannot agree on price. Since the proposed form of the transaction is an exchange of stock, the business and financial characteristics of both firms must be evaluated in terms of separate and combined values of their equity interests.

Loeffler Tool, Inc.

In an attempt to structure a leveraged buyout of Loeffler Tool, a machine tools division of a large international conglomerate, the would–be principals wrestle with a host of difficult valuation issues. And the inherent volatility of this industry just exacerbates the situation, particularly with regard to estimating future cash flows.

Flanihan Engineering and Construction, Inc.

A large, national transportation engineering and construction services firm, Flanihan Engineering and Construction, Inc., has managed its business development and contract services work very successfully, but it has looked at working capital as a residual. With a sudden ballooning of receivables and payables, and a new CFO, the need for active management of these activities is now more apparent. One complication in using industry norms to guide working capital decisions is that this company is in more than one industry. And as with all such policy decisions, it is not entirely clear what the costs and benefits are if new policies are adopted.

O.L. Kimps, Inc.

While understandably distracted by the demands of financing a number of major, strategic acquisitions recently, O.L. Kimps, a large international book publisher, has lost sight of the need to manage working capital—and cash. The acquisitions have only compounded the problem with additional, largely unknown, working capital requirements. What is clear is the resulting large swings in cash, and the concern such liquidity issues raise for senior management.

The Ware Company

Can a company generate too much cash? If it does, what should it do with it? These aren't questions that most companies have to deal with, but the Ware Company, a catalog retailer of men's and women's apparel, could be facing such a quandary in the very near future. In short, it has used the cash it has earned in the last few years to invest in state–of–the–art technology, pay off both short–term and long–term debt, and even buy back some of its common stock. Yet it still has ample cash, and is expecting to continue to produce a steady stream of new funds for the foreseeable future.

Woods of New Hampshire, Inc.

Woods of New Hampshire, Inc., mills various hardwoods and sells most of its product in pre–packaged home building kits. Without some formal inventory control systems, quantities can easily balloon and profitability suffer. But simply adopting modern production–inventory philosophies by no means assures optimal inventory investments. By delving into all the details of implementing such a system, this case allows for some quantification of what benefits may occur from a more disciplined approach to inventory investment.

Feedback

Writing good cases is a real art, and I do not have this all figured out yet, to be sure. I do work on my cases regularly to improve where I can, and, therefore, I not only welcome feedback, I encourage it. For example, there are certain pieces of information that I have specifically included or specifically excluded because I felt it made for a better case and stretched my students a little more as a result. These judgments are the "art" form in such writing, and they produce the uncertainties of knowing what is really best. I appreciate other perspectives; please send your comments to:

M. J. Murray
Economics and Finance Dept.
Winona State University
Winona, MN 55987

Contents

Case 6 Mosher Pumps, Inc.   43

Case 7 Tenneson Property Investors, Inc.   47

Part III Cost of Capital   55

Case 8 Mobile Energy, Inc.   57

Case 9 Northern Woods Campers, Inc.   65

Part IV Financial Policy   71

Case 10 O'Malley Steel, Inc.   73

Part I
Financial Analysis

Case 1
Servais Stores, Inc.

His regular, early morning reading of *The Wall Street Journal* used to be pleasant duty for the former CFO, but now it was just a daily reminder of his company's continued financial difficulties. Obviously, 1989 had been a disastrous year for Servais Stores, the operator and franchiser of Time/Saver convenience stores. Several months had passed since Robert DeYoung, now the CEO of Servais Stores, had had to deal with the firm's anxious creditors and disgruntled investors, and as promised in those meetings, the company had made real progress in conserving cash, primarily by suspending expansion efforts and selling off some of its stores. But in spite of the improved cash flows just reported in first quarter results, the price of the company's stock continued to sink and the major rating agencies once again downgraded its debt to "B". From the options data Mr. DeYoung was studying from the Pacific Exchange, it was clear that the market was betting against him in his efforts to turn the company around.

The economy was still expanding, particularly in the Sunbelt region where Servais Stores operated most of its stores. The industry, though intensely competitive now, was still growing, both in the number of new stores and in sales per store. The company's recent expansion into Europe and Japan seemed threatened, however; it was all but certain that Servais Stores would have to sell out to its joint venture partner, Oxford Petroleum, its share of last year's successful acquisition of the Gas 'n Go chain of convenience stores in southern California. In short, the tremendous expansion the company had engineered over the last six years (see EXHIBIT 1), most of which Mr. DeYoung himself had structured, was beginning to come undone—but bankruptcy? Surely the market was wrong here.

As the rest of the offices began to gain light and life, Mr. DeYoung called in his secretary and asked her to schedule an all–day session with his senior staff on Monday to discuss these issues. For the first time in his career, Robert DeYoung suddenly felt out of touch with his business.

Company and Industry

Servais Stores, Inc., was formed in 1980 with the merger of two smaller chains of convenience stores in northern Florida, principally in Jacksonville and Tallahassee, although their operating histories dated back to the early sixties. Less than six months later, the corporation acquired a larger, though struggling, convenience store subsidiary of a large regional grocer which owned over 600 convenience stores in central and southern Florida. By 1983, Servais Stores operated or franchised almost 1,200 outlets in Florida, Georgia, and Alabama. Another major acquisition in 1985 of a Texas oil company's stores in that state more than doubled the number of stores in operation, and following that were additional store openings and acquisitions in Arizona and Southern California in the late 1980s.

The Time/Saver stores sell the typical fast food and beverage items, tobacco products, groceries, magazines, and health and beauty items; over three–fourths of the outlets also sell gasoline. More recently,

---

Sources: Data and information based on various publications, including S&P Stock Reports, S&P Industry Surveys, RMA Annual Statement Studies.

several stores were remodeled to expand their floor space for video rentals, financial services (automated teller machines, money orders, bill paying centers, etc.), and mail/shipping services (express drop–offs, shipping materials and packaging services, and mailboxes). The "average" store in the Time/Saver chain grosses about $750,000, although profits range from $650,000 – $950,000. After–tax profits are about 2 percent of sales.

The convenience store industry grew rapidly in the 1980s, and even gained momentum in the later half of the decade, seemingly fueled by the growth of "superstore" groceries (30,000–60,000 sq. ft., $8–10mm gross sales). Consumers apparently were choosing either price or convenience, at the expense of traditional grocery stores. Also in the late 1980s, the convenience store segment of the industry became dominated by major oil companies who had the financial strength to expand and upgrade their holdings. The resulting competition was the most intense traditional grocery–based chains had ever experienced. Competition took the form primarily of upgrading and relocating facilities, from dingy (and dangerous?) intercity "corner" sites to bright and attractive, high–volume outlets along major arteries. Companies like Servais Stores responded with acquisitions, and in some of their existing stores, expanded services in renovated, though not really upgraded, facilities. For Servais Stores, the video rental business was enormously profitable, while the financial and mail/shipping services made the Time/Saver stores more unique and all encompassing, thereby allowing the company to hold market share. However, the efforts to keep pace resulted in heavy debt loads, declining profitability and cash flow problems. The widely reported financial difficulties of Southland ("7–11"), Dairy Mart Convenience, and even National Convenience Stores serve to illustrate that Servais Stores was not alone in its financial distress. The general deterioration in its financial condition is apparent from the company's financial statements over the last few years (see EXHIBITS 2 and 3).

The Company's Current Condition

Early Monday morning, the meeting opened with Al Costa, senior vice–president of operations, confirming the nature of the competition in the industry and concluding that, if the company was to continue to be a major player, expanded services and relocations needed to be high priorities in the next two to three years. Patricia Cline, vice–president of marketing, followed with a very optimistic assessment of the contribution of the video business and expanded services to profitability and market share. The only problem was that too few stores had converted. For example, she stated that for about $60,000 per store, upgraded outlets could produce 25 percent higher sales. And these more efficient outlets typically produced operating income margins of 4 percent, thereby almost doubling profitability, and having a payback of as little as eight years. Finally, she noted that more aggressive promotion and perhaps price competition would be necessary to keep pace in many of the major markets in which the company had stores. Hermann Lindner, vice–president of finance, spoke next, and painted a very different picture. Growth and upgrades had come at a price. Debt levels were dangerously high, even in a highly levered industry (see EXHIBIT 4), cash was low, sales were being realized only with huge investments in fixed assets, and profit margins were being eroded by rapidly escalating expenses. He went on to state that in 1989 the company was barely able to meet its contractual obligations to creditors and that without some significant program of expense control the company could be technically insolvent by year end. His comments were very sobering. Each of the participants looked into the eyes of the others and realized that they were all having the same thought — was the current situation even salvageable? In particular, was six to nine months long enough to alter the company's current path? This certainly wasn't the first time Robert DeYoung had had these thoughts, but they took on a special urgency now. He took a deep breath and suggested a short break.

Alternatives

After a brief recess, Mr. DeYoung began with the subject of bankruptcy specifically. Was it inevitable? "No" said Mr. Lindner, "but it is imminent." The discussion then centered on whether the company should use the next few months to pursue actions that would avoid bankruptcy at all costs, or to develop a reorganization plan that would better prepare itself for Chapter 11. At this point Mr. DeYoung noted that the $260 million bank credit agreement it had negotiated last year with a syndicate of banks, lead by Marine National Banks of Florida, was probably going to be the trigger, since another $65 million principal payment was due in six months. A major infusion of cash should come from the sale of a group of 37 stores to Oxford Petroleum for about $45 million. Other sales would take some time to realize, and bring considerably less per store. For example, Mr. Lindner noted that the "average" Time/Saver store was now producing only about $15,000 profit, and that with even 70 percent debt financing (at, say, 9 percent, 5.4 percent after–tax), the investment value of these stores wasn't much more than $200,000. Finally, Patricia Cline offered that internally generated funds would be scarce over the next six to nine months, since sales were projected to be essentially flat. With more aggressive price promotion and merchandise–based marketing, she believed growth could reach 10–15 percent. Operating income margin however, would continue dropping, from 3.5 percent currently projected to about 3 percent, due to both lower prices and higher expenses.

It was early evening now and everybody was starting to get a little tired. More thought and probably some modeling needed to be done before the group could properly assess the alternatives. Mr. DeYoung set another all day session for next Monday, and was quite clear about wanting to develop some fairly concrete plans soon thereafter.

Discussion Questions

1. Based on an analysis of Servais Stores' financial statements, what are their strengths and weaknesses? What do you think was behind the rating agencies' downgrading of the company's debt?

2. What does an analysis of the company's cash flows reveal? What is meant by "free cash flows"? Is there a liquidity problem over the next six to nine months?

3. What should the banks do about the $260 million note?

4. In general, what are the advantages and disadvantages (to the company) of alternative remedies for firms that fail? What strategy should Servais Stores pursue?

5. The company clearly can't "stay the course." What will 1990 results look like under this base case scenario? What type and magnitude of adjustments can be made in the next six to nine months to improve the picture?

6. Within a two to three year time frame, what should Servais Stores do to make the company healthier financially and still be competitive? Develop pro forma financial statements for the next two years for these "solutions."

7. What additional information would be useful for this analysis?

Exhibit 1
Sales and Store Growth
1984–1989

	Sales		Number of Stores	
	($mm)	% change	(#)	% change
1989	$3,495	31.5	4,685	14.9
1988	2,657	14.7	4,077	16.3
1987	2,317	8.8	3,507	4.0
1986	2,129	25.7	3,372	26.3
1985	1,694	63.7	2,669	118.6
1984	1,035	37.3	1,221	2.3

Exhibit 2
Statements of Operations
1985–1989

($mm) Year Ended April 30	1985	1986	1987	1988	1989
Revenues	1,694	2,129	2,317	2,657	3,495
– Operating Expenses	1,591	1,982	2,143	2,462	3,324
Operating Income	103	147	174	195	171
– Depreciation	25	36	44	59	79
EBIT	78	111	130	136	92
– Interest Expense	24	41	48	64	102
Earnings Before Taxes	54	70	82	72	(10)
+ Other Income	5	1	12	16	37
Net Before Taxes	59	71	94	88	27
– Income Taxes	26	31	45	33	12
NET INCOME	33	40	49	55	15

Exhibit 3
Statements of Financial Condition
1985–1989

($mm) Year Ended April 30	1985	1986	1987	1988	1989
Assets					
Cash	22	20	25	44	39
Other Current Assets	154	254	334	336	370
Total Current Assets	176	274	359	380	409
Long–Term Assets	404	579	778	1,156	1,636
TOTAL ASSETS	580	853	1,137	1,536	2,045
Liabilities and Equity					
Total Current Liabilities	115	185	169	281	350
Other Long–Term Liabilities	5	8	33	42	120
Long–Term Debt	269	383	537	844	1,104
Other Long–Term Capital	68	79	88	85	191
Common Equity	123	198	310	284	280
Total Invested Capital	460	660	935	1,213	1,575
TOTAL LIABILITIES AND EQUITY	580	853	1,137	1,536	2,045

Exhibit 4
Industry Financial Ratios
1988 and 1989

	1988	1989
Current Ratio	1.0	1.1
Cash Ratio	0.3	0.3
Sales/Net Fixed Assets	8.1	9.6
Sales/Total Assets	4.3	4.5
Debt to Total Assets	73.5	71.5
EBIT/Interest	1.7	2.1
Pretax Margin on Sales	0.9%	1.3%
Pretax Margin on Assets	3.1%	5.4%
Pretax Margin on Equity	13.8%	20.0%

Case 2
Ohio, Indiana and Central States Corporation

His opening remarks seemed quite positive this year. At least that was the reaction of Frank Madigan, a 15–year veteran of these annual retreats, and the company's treasurer. These affairs had often seemed like therapy sessions in the past. But the picture painted by Ohio, Indiana and Central States Corporation's CEO Geoffrey Smith was notably upbeat, as he spoke of markedly improved efficiency and profitability, a safety record now among the best in the industry, and a future of interesting challenges and opportunities. This hardly seemed like a meeting of railroad executives. But this company was on the move, so to speak. From its rebirth in mid–1990 as a publicly traded company, it has grown increasingly healthy, both operationally and financially, and now enjoys market valuations which approach those of the better Class I railroads. But what was in the back of Frank Madigan's mind, and probably the others in the room with him, was the ever–present possibility of a takeover.

State of the Industry

The next speaker was Joseph Fleming, a railroad industry consultant. He made several major points in his presentation. First, he stated that the Staggers Rail Act of 1980, which partially deregulated rail rates and services, had literally transformed the industry, and in just over a decade. It had spawned greater competition and thereby efficiency, track and equipment investments had surged during this period, and profitability, better service, and lower rates were all characteristics of this new environment. Other indicators of a now healthier rail industry were greater cooperation among railroads with connections and track usage, significantly increased intermodal traffic, with both truck and barge shipping, and a dramatic reduction in the number of accidents, due largely to capital investments and improvements. Second, he noted that the industry has become much more concentrated. For example, the 13 largest railroads now account for 91 percent of total rail industry revenues, with the industry's five largest (Union Pacific, Burlington Northern, CSX, Norfolk Southern, and Consolidated Rail) claiming two–thirds of total revenues. And this consolidation is continuing, albeit at a slower pace. Regional carriers are the primary targets, although there are signs that even the second tier of the Class I roads are vulnerable. The most tangible evidence of this is Union Pacific Corporation's recent purchase of Chicago & North Western's stock, giving it approximately 30 percent interest in C & NW.

The third point made by Mr. Fleming was the trend toward increased flexibility in the shipping business. This is something the industry has had to learn. But through investments in new, more adaptable car platforms, terminal and transloading facilities, microelectronics and telecommunications, and the aforementioned cooperation among rail lines, today's railroads can offer highly individualized shipping

---

Sources: Data and information based on various publications, including S&P Stock Reports, S&P Industry Surveys, S&P Analyst's Handbook, U.S. Industrial Outlook.

and transportation services to U.S. industry and agriculture. Finally, he stated that the outlook for the industry was for modest, though profitable, expansion. In real terms, volume was expected to grow by only 1 to 1–1/2 percent per year for the next several years, but revenues could increase by 4–7 percent, depending on the type of freight. And with operating costs declining, largely as a result of negotiated reductions in the size and function of train crews, profitability should continue to improve. Of course, a strong national economy was a fundamental assumption in this outlook, but this seemed to be a perfectly valid supposition.

Ohio, Indiana and Central States

After a break for lunch, President Ray Janiszewski presented the 1992 financial results (see EXHIBITS 1 and 2), and then provided a framework for the discussions which would follow. In particular, he noted a strong market reaction following the release of these improved 1992 data and suggested that continued success and independence would be contingent on managing those factors which the financial markets view as important in determining the level and growth of earnings. Without this focus, the company likely would be undervalued in the marketplace, and this would be a red flag to potential acquirers. As Mr. Janiszewski put it, "This would be like letting blood into a sea of hungry sharks."

From an operational perspective, he identified several positive developments: a) the opening and expansion of facilities of some of the company's major customers; b) an alliance with the Jensen Company, a leading motor carrier of truckload freight, for joint handling of intermodal freight from several of the railroad's key terminals; c) the completion of the new $6 million intermodal yard near Evansville; and d) a significant 10 percent growth in ton–miles in the past year due, about equally, to longer average hauls and larger average tonnage shipped.

Some of the major financial issues of this past year which will affect future results as well were: a) labor savings from the recent crew–reduction agreement; b) the costs related to 1992's rail strike and Hurricane Andrew; c) a one–time $10 million charge against 1992 earnings for retirement expenses and asset revaluations; d) the $45 million of capital improvements in 1992, which should grow to $55–$60 million per year over the next couple of years; e) the institution of a $0.50/share dividend payment, and f) the continuation in the shift from debt to equity capital.

For these and other reasons, Mr. Janiszewski stated that the 1993–95 planning period, the object of this retreat, was expected to produce 4–5 percent revenue growth on the low end to 7–8 percent on the high side, some additional though modest improvements in the company's operating expense ratio, lower degrees of financial leverage, and other unspecified improvements in operations and finances which this group was expected to identify and, "to make it so," as he put it.

With this basic structure defined, the plan now was to break into discussion groups and determine what could be done, what effects any resulting decisions would have on reported results, and most importantly, what the absolute and relative market valuations would be through this planning period. As a guide to this effort, various accounting and market norms are provided for the Class I railroads in EXHIBITS 3 and 4, and for specific competitors and like firms in EXHIBITS 5 and 6.

Competitor/Like Firm Backgrounds

As some basis for evaluating the data for other comparable rail companies, a brief description of their systems and activities is provided. The principal competitors to Ohio, Indiana and Central States (OICS) are Kansas City Southern and Chicago and North Western. Similar firms, that have remained public, are Florida East Coast and Wisconsin Central Transportation.

Kansas City Southern

This regional railroad, with some 1,700 miles of track, is about two–thirds the size of Ohio, Indiana and Central States, yet generates 10–15 percent higher revenues because of a successful, well–diversified financial services subsidiary (which provides record–keeping services for mutual funds, security transfer services and portfolio accounting, claims processing services, custom software for the insurance industry, investment management and advisory services, etc.). Of the 12.2 billion ton–miles of freight it hauled in 1991, coal accounted for one–third of the total, followed by intermodal (15 percent), chemicals (13 percent), and petroleum (10 percent). By contrast, the Ohio, Indiana and Central States railroad handles chemicals and agricultural products primarily, but does compete directly with Kansas City Southern for these other products.

Chicago & North Western

Another direct competitor, the Chicago & North Western, is more than twice the size in trackage and ton–miles of freight hauled, but yields only 85 percent of Ohio, Indiana and Central States' revenues per ton–mile. Almost two–thirds of its loads are interchanged with Union Pacific, and by no coincidence, Union Pacific has purchased about 30 percent of its common shares outstanding since C & NW went public at the end of 1991. If this company remains public, it will be in name only.

Florida East Coast

As its name suggests, Florida East Coast railroad operates along the 400+ mile stretch between Jacksonville and Miami, and is about 30 percent of the size of Ohio, Indiana and Central States. Its real estate development subsidiary is quite prosperous, generating over 15 percent of total revenues. As the economy continues to improve, the future looks bright for both activities of this company. It does not compete directly with OICS, but is one of the few smaller Class I railroads that has not gone private or merged with another Class I road.

Wisconsin Central Transportation

Also remaining independent is Wisconsin Central, the largest regional railroad in the U.S. It operates on over 2,000 miles of track in Wisconsin and the Upper Peninsula of Michigan, eastern Minnesota, and northern Illinois. The heart of this company is with the paper producers of the Fox River Valley in Wisconsin. Its 10 largest customers from this area make up half of total revenues. Almost two–thirds of revenues are concentrated in just 25 shippers.

In terms of return on assets, the basic earning power of railroads, Ohio, Indiana and Central States has been the best producer of this group. It also has the most diversified freight and customer base. And like most rail companies today, it has transformed itself from a railroad to a transportation services company, with the word services underscored. With the agricultural and industrial economy of the heartland as its base, OICS has been dealt a strong hand. But it will need strong, creative management to realize its potential, not something usually associated with railroads.

Discussion Questions

1. Conduct a complete financial analysis of the company and identify its strengths and weaknesses.

2. How does Ohio, Indiana and Central States Corporation differ from the industry in terms of market valuations? Explain these differences. In other words, what factors contribute to higher market valuations?

3. What insights/information can be gained by the "spreadsheet approach" (comparing the subject firm to just a few competitor/like firms), in terms of performance and market valuations?

4. Project Ohio, Indiana and Central States Corporation's financial statements (including cash flows) over the next three years. Analyze the effects on market valuations of varying the key assumptions in the financial projections.

5. If the goal of this firm was indeed to maximize the value of its stock, and to discourage would–be acquirers at the same time, what would be your recommendations for managing the key variables?

6. Think about what type of substantial, and presently unanticipated, industry developments could throw a monkey wrench into the forecast. Should planning efforts account for these in any way?

7. What additional information would be useful for this analysis?

Exhibit 1
Statements of Operations
1989–1992

($mm) Year Ended December 31	1989	1990	1991	1992
Revenues	399	544	550	547
– Operating Expenses	303	389	384	364
Operating Income	96	155	166	183
– Depreciation	16	22	20	22
EBIT	80	133	146	161
– Interest Expense	73	76	60	46
Earnings Before Taxes	7	57	86	115
+ Other Income	7	12	10	18
Net Before Taxes	14	69	96	133
– Income Taxes	4	23	31	37
NET INCOME	10	46	65	96

Exhibit 2
Statements of Financial Condition
1989–1992

($mm) Year Ended December 31	1989	1990	1991	1992
Assets				
Cash	27	14	33	35
Other Current Assets	209	160	147	130
Total Current Assets	236	174	180	165
Long–Term Assets	929	978	1,004	1,041
TOTAL ASSETS	1,165	1,152	1,184	1,206
Liabilities and Equity				
Total Current Liabilities	309	218	183	168
Other Long–Term Liabilities	83	160	155	0
Long–Term Debt	538	486	414	367
Other Long–Term Capital	236	160	172	332
Common Equity	(1)	128	260	339
Total Invested Capital	773	774	846	1,038
TOTAL LIABILITIES AND EQUITY	1,165	1,152	1,184	1,206

Exhibit 3
Class I Railroad Industry Norms
1989–1992

Accounting Data	1989	1990	1991	1992
Current Ratio	0.9	0.9	0.8	–
Total Asset Turnover	0.5	0.5	0.3	–
Debt/Capital	.39	.43	.38	–
Equity/Assets	.34	.32	.33	–
Operating Expense Ratio	.23	.21	.19	–
Dividend Payout Ratio	.39	.39	n/m	–
Pretax Profit Margin	5.5%	7.8%	0.7%	–
Pretax Return on Assets	3.8%	3.6%	0.3%	–
Pretax Return on Equity	11.7%	10.5%	0.7%	–
Market and Per Share Data				
Price/Earnings	13x	12x	11x	–
Market/Book Values	1.4	1.3	1.5	–

Exhibit 4
Price, Dividends, and Earnings Data Per Share:
S&P 500, Railroad Industry, and Ohio, Indiana & C.S.

		S&P 500			Railroads			Ohio, Indiana & C.S.		
		Price	Divid	Earn	Price	Divid	Earn	Price	Divid	Earn
1988	4th	277.72	2.48	5.62	171.89	1.58	5.32	–	–	–
1989	1st	294.87	2.50	6.74	179.19	1.47	3.21	–	–	–
	2nd	317.98	2.86	6.48	191.26	1.41	4.50	–	–	–
	3rd	349.15	2.83	4.85	211.16	1.57	4.53	–	–	–
	4th	353.40	2.86	4.80	214.24	1.74	1.82	–	–	–
1990	1st	339.94	2.77	5.54	211.86	1.60	2.58	–	–	0.40
	2nd	358.02	3.21	6.07	218.10	1.61	4.69	10.00	–	0.31
	3rd	306.05	3.00	5.33	179.82	1.69	4.70	7.88	–	0.25
	4th	330.22	3.12	4.40	197.93	1.89	4.57	8.00	–	0.35
1991	1st	375.22	2.79	5.14	213.30	1.89	2.88	10.75	–	0.43
	2nd	371.16	3.24	4.54	237.41	1.82	0.63	15.63	–	0.35
	3rd	387.86	3.13	3.74	276.19	1.88	0.25	18.25	–	0.41
	4th	417.09	3.04	2.55	313.27	2.08	(7.31)	19.38	–	0.45
1992	1st	403.69	2.91	5.36	301.33	1.97	4.43	23.13	–	0.50
	2nd	408.14	3.24	5.40	317.62	1.98	1.53	21.25	0.10	0.40
	3rd	417.80	3.20	4.73	309.51	2.07	3.90	18.75	0.10	0.41
	4th	431.71	3.03	3.61	342.81	2.23	7.65	23.88	0.15	0.52

Exhibit 5
Competitor Financial Data
1989–1992

Kansas City Southern Industries

($mm) Year Ended December 31	1989	1990	1991	1992
REVENUES	497	528	610	741
OPERATING INCOME	137	137	156	200
Depreciation	55	50	58	74
Interest Expense	30	31	32	33
Other Income, Net	6	6	8	(2)
NET BEFORE TAXES	58	62	74	91
Income Taxes	21	21	28	27
NET INCOME	37	41	46	64
Cash	106	87	44	15
TOTAL CURRENT ASSETS	252	239	232	246
LONG–TERM ASSETS	713	795	860	1,002
TOTAL ASSETS	965	1,034	1,092	1,248
TOTAL CURRENT LIABILITIES	200	172	201	219
Long–Term Debt	283	345	317	387
Common Equity	332	369	405	456
TOTAL INVESTED CAPITAL	708	801	829	1,029

Chicago & North Western Holdings

($mm) Year Ended December 31	1989	1990	1991	1992
REVENUES	–	–	979	–
OPERATING INCOME	–	–	278	–
Depreciation	–	–	67	–
Interest Expense	–	–	120	–
Other Income, Net	–	–	(104)	–
NET BEFORE TAXES	–	–	(13)	–
Income Taxes	–	–	(5)	–
NET INCOME	–	–	(8)	–
Cash	–	–	61	–
TOTAL CURRENT ASSETS	–	–	264	–
LONG–TERM ASSETS	–	–	1,853	–
TOTAL ASSETS	–	–	2,117	–
TOTAL CURRENT LIABILITIES	–	–	328	–
Long–Term Debt	–	–	1,315	–
Common Equity	–	–	95	–
TOTAL INVESTED CAPITAL	–	–	1,410	–

Exhibit 5 (cont.)
Florida East Coast

($mm) Year Ended December 31	1989	1990	1991	1992
REVENUES	168	170	167	–
OPERATING INCOME	50	45	37	–
Depreciation	15	17	18	–
Interest Expense	0	0	0	–
Other Income, Net	27	21	26	–
NET BEFORE TAXES	62	49	45	–
Income Taxes	22	18	16	–
NET INCOME	40	31	29	–
Cash	36	46	42	–
TOTAL CURRENT ASSETS	86	87	83	–
LONG–TERM ASSETS	510	536	565	–
TOTAL ASSETS	596	623	648	–
TOTAL CURRENT LIABILITIES	36	34	45	–
Long–Term Debt	0	0	0	–
Common Equity	442	469	483	–
TOTAL INVESTED CAPITAL	551	581	595	–

Wisconsin Central Transportation

($mm) Year Ended December 31	1989	1990	1991	1992
REVENUES	101	113	114	–
OPERATING INCOME	31	31	28	–
Depreciation	8	8	8	–
Interest Expense	16	15	11	–
Other Income, Net	2	4	5	–
NET BEFORE TAXES	9	12	14	–
Income Taxes	3	4	5	–
NET INCOME	6	8	9	–
Cash	3	16	3	–
TOTAL CURRENT ASSETS	33	52	35	–
LONG–TERM ASSETS	164	168	193	–
TOTAL ASSETS	197	220	228	–
TOTAL CURRENT LIABILITIES	52	56	40	–
Long–Term Debt	118	119	96	–
Common Equity	22	29	74	–
TOTAL INVESTED CAPITAL	143	155	181	–

Exhibit 6
Competitor and Like Firm Per Share and Market Data
1989–1992

		1989	1990	1991	1992
Earnings/Share	– Ohio, Ind. & C.S.	0.09	1.31	1.64	1.70
	– Kansas City So.	1.78	1.98	2.16	2.80
	– Chicago & N.W.	n/a	(3.61)	(3.42)	(0.75)
	– Florida East Coast	4.28	3.39	3.21	3.10
	– Wisconsin Central	1.44	1.89	1.58	1.68
Dividends/Share	– Ohio, Ind. & C.S.	–	–	–	.50
	– Kansas City So.	.54	.54	.54	.54
	– Chicago & N.W.	–	–	–	–
	– Florida East Coast	.40	.40	.40	.40
	– Wisconsin Central	–	–	–	–
Price/Earnings	– Ohio, Ind. & C.S.	n/a	7x	9x	12x
	– Kansas City So.	12x	11x	11x	13x
	– Chicago & N.W.	–	–	n/a	n/a
	– Florida East Coast	15x	15x	14x	14x
	– Wisconsin Central	n/a	n/a	12x	17x
Market/Book	– Ohio, Ind. & C.S.	n/a	2.4	2.5	2.6
	– Kansas City So.	1.4	1.5	1.5	1.2
	– Chicago & N.W.	–	–	n/m	n/m
	– Florida East Coast	1.4	1.0	0.8	–
	– Wisconsin Central	n/a	n/a	1.7	–

Case 3
Manchester Inns, Inc.

"Bill, I think this company is stuck in neutral. We have essentially the same number of motels that we had five years ago, our financial statements have been uniformly underwhelming over that period, and the stock has traded within the same narrow range for five to six years. I realize we've been battling a recession and an overbuilt industry of late—and I applaud our efforts, truly—but I feel like I'm mired in that muck we built our unit in Port Everglades in. There are opportunities out there, and I'd like to get back to the fun part of this business."

V. Chang, the chairman and CEO of Manchester Inns, was musing to his old friend and partner, William Townsend, the company's senior vice–president of finance, at one of their regular biweekly breakfast meetings. "Yes, I've had the same thoughts, but it's been tough keeping this company going the last couple of years. How do we break out of this?" So went Bill Townsend's response, and the nature and tone of their discussion that morning. Both men were now keen on creating some movement for the company.

The Company's Current Position

There was no set agenda at their meetings—that was one of the rules—but they both understood the cumulative nature of these meetings, and both had taken some extra time prior to this subsequent meeting to try to figure out where the company was, and what they could do to change the situation.

Mr. Townsend led off with his analysis of the company's financial statements (see EXHIBITS 1 and 2), which pretty much confirmed Mr. Chang's observation from two weeks ago. That is, there had been little change in the income statements or balance sheets for several years. Additionally, he noted how closely, and in some cases favorably, the company's various ratios compared to the industry norms (EXHIBIT 3). Yet, the firm's performance in the financial markets (EXHIBIT 4) could be considered lackluster at best. "You know we can tweak any one of these numbers or ratios a little bit if we really tried, but there has to be a more fundamental change if we are to create some true movement," Townsend concluded.

"Well, I've been thinking about that," responded Chang, "and I feel the key is to get a more favorable rate on our debt. I realize this is a 'Catch–22,' but I believe this is where we need to focus our efforts. At what rate could we refinance those convertible bonds (280,000, $1,000 bonds, convertible to 40 common shares) now?"

"The yield now is 10.7 percent for 15 to 20 year bonds with 'BB' rating, a proxy for our current creditworthiness, and they now carry a 11.25 percent rate," replied Townsend. "Even with 15 to 16 years remaining, I don't think that that is a large enough difference to pay for the refinancing. The call premium is an extra year's interest, and it would probably cost us at least $2 to 3 million to issue new debt," he continued. "But, I'll look at the possibilities and let you know."

Sources: Data and information based on various publications, including S&P Stock Reports and RMA Annual Statement Studies.

"Do that," said Chang, "but I was thinking that if we could make some substantive changes in our ratios we could get even the 'A' rate (interest rate on S&P 'A'–rated bonds). From what studies I've read, the more critical ratios for these rate differentials are debt ratios, interest coverage, and return on assets. Let's jump start this thing by selling some assets."

"But we have good quality assets now; we've worked hard on that over the years," said Townsend. "They're in good locations and their productivity (EXHIBIT 5) is fairly uniform. Their average market value is approximately $4 million, ranging perhaps from $2.5 to $5.5 million, but they could be worth more when the economy improves and the overhang in this industry works itself off—for example, we are projecting an 8 to 10 percent improvement in operating income for each of the next couple of years. I'd hate to sell now if we don't have to."

"Aren't interest rates just going to be higher then?" countered Chang. "The last time I looked, the yield curve was clearly showing this, but again, let's look into it and determine what the possibilities are (see EXHIBITS 6 and 7). By the way, I'll be on vacation for our next meeting, so let's pick it up again after that."

Discussion Questions

1. How would CEO Chang's idea get the company out of "neutral," as he characterizes their current plight?

2. Estimate the market value of the $280 million in convertible bonds. Is there a chance that they will convert into equity anytime soon? In other words, what is the breakeven point on these securities and what would produce the circumstances to achieve this?

3. Estimate the forward interest rates, first on Treasury securities, and then in terms of what "BBB" and "A" rated corporates would yield.

4. Assuming that the company would continue to pay the "BB" rate, does it make sense to refund the bond issue now? One year from now? Two years?

5. Not knowing for sure whether the company would qualify for "BBB" or an "A" rate, how many inns should be sold to start the process in motion? Or, should the company just wait until they are worth more? How long?

6. Prepare pro formas, two to three years out, for any alternatives that seem feasible.

7. What additional information would be useful for this analysis?

Exhibit 1
Statements of Operations
1986–1991

($mm) Year Ended December 31	1986	1987	1988	1989	1990	1991
Revenues	177	174	192	206	226	243
– Operating Expenses	116	115	124	134	151	159
Operating Income	61	59	68	72	75	84
– Depreciation	29	30	30	31	32	32
EBIT	32	29	38	41	43	52
– Interest Expense	42	42	42	42	40	38
Earnings Before Taxes	(10)	(13)	(4)	(1)	3	14
+ Other Income	19	17	13	12	9	(3)
Net Before Taxes	9	4	9	11	12	11
– Income Taxes	5	1	4	5	10	10
NET INCOME	4	3	5	6	2	1

Exhibit 2
Statements of Financial Condition
1986–1991

($mm) Year Ended December 31	1986	1987	1988	1989	1990	1991
Assets						
Cash	38	41	33	12	14	8
Other Current Assets	17	17	18	16	20	13
Total Current Assets	55	58	51	28	34	21
Long–Term Assets	568	534	551	549	553	554
TOTAL ASSETS	623	592	602	577	587	575
Liabilities and Equity						
Total Current Liabilities	40	43	65	45	52	56
Other Long–Term Liabilities	50	39	30	29	27	22
Long–Term Debt	382	369	361	351	342	316
Other Long–Term Capital	33	30	29	29	37	51
Common Equity	118	111	117	123	129	130
Total Invested Capital	533	510	507	503	508	497
TOTAL LIABILITIES AND EQUITY	623	592	602	577	587	575

Exhibit 3
Industry Financial Ratios
1987–1991

	1987	1988	1989	1990	1991
Current Ratio	0.6	0.6	0.7	0.6	0.6
Sales/Assets	0.7	0.7	0.7	0.7	0.6
Total Debt/Assets	.78	.80	.79	.79	.80
Long–Term Debt/Total Capital	.68	.70	.68	.70	.68
EBIT/Interest	1.5	1.4	1.4	1.5	1.6
Pretax Return on Revenues	2.7%	2.4%	3.0%	2.6%	3.5%
Pretax Return on Assets	2.5%	2.0%	1.6%	1.7%	2.7%
Pretax Return on Equity	14.8%	12.3%	10.8%	11.8%	15.2%

Exhibit 4
Per Share and Market Data
1986–1991

	1986	1987	1988	1989	1990	1991
Earnings/Share	$0.30	0.24	0.36	0.43	0.17	0.11
Dividends/Share	$0.00	0.00	0.00	0.00	0.00	0.00
Book Value/Share	$8.85	8.88	8.42	8.82	10.97	14.30
Price–High	$16.750	14.625	14.875	18.500	17.875	15.500
–Low	$11.250	9.875	11.750	13.000	11.250	10.000

Exhibit 5
Average Productivity of Manchester Inns
1988–1991

	1988	1989	1990	1991
Number of Inns	198	207	210	212
Number of Rooms	110	110	110	110
Average Occupancy	61.3%	65.5%	66.0%	64.8%
Average Daily Revenue	$36.4	$38.7	$40.9	$43.1

Exhibit 6
Historical Interest Rates
1982–1992

Year	Corporate			Government	
	A	BBB	BB	20 Yr.	6 Mo.
1992e	8.90%	9.20%	10.70%	7.60%	4.30%
1991	9.38	10.48	11.69	8.03	6.12
1990	10.03	10.77	13.03	8.77	8.11
1989	10.08	10.48	11.75	8.74	8.79
1988	10.37	10.83	11.16	9.02	8.17
1987	10.16	10.79	–	8.94	7.58
1986	9.79	10.54	–	8.37	7.36
1985	11.35	12.16	–	10.54	9.47
1984	13.24	13.95	–	12.57	11.71
1983	12.01	12.68	–	11.09	10.24
1982	13.66	15.16	–	12.25	12.07

Exhibit 7
Treasury Yield Curve

		YTM			YTM
NOW	(1st Qtr, 1992)	3.65%	+ 6	(1st, 1998)	7.06%
+ 0.5	(3rd Qtr, 1992)	4.29	+ 6.5		7.10
+ 1	(1st, 1993)	4.67	+ 7	(1st, 1999)	7.28
+ 1.5		5.17	+ 7.5		7.33
+ 2	(1st, 1994)	5.46	+ 8	(1st, 2000)	7.37
+ 2.5		5.82	+ 8.5		7.40
+ 3	(1st, 1995)	6.07	+ 9	(1st, 2001)	7.42
+ 3.5		6.36	+ 9.5		7.49
+ 4	(1st, 1996)	6.58	+ 10	(1st, 2002)	7.55
+ 4.5		6.72			
+ 5	(1st, 1997)	6.87	+ 15	(1st, 2007)	7.90
+ 5.5		6.98	+ 20	(1st, 2012)	7.92

Case 4
Riordan Industries, Inc.

Robert Gillette, Riordan Industries' vice–president for development, opened the meeting with the observation that the financial markets had reacted favorably to its decision a little over a year ago to divest itself of the machine tool controls, disk–drive test equipment, and capacitor business lines, in spite of the $3 million hit to 1992 earnings. The recovery of its farm equipment division helped too, but Mr. Gillette was reading the markets' reaction as an approval of the overall strategic plan adopted by the company the previous year. It was this plan, precisely, that this annual review meeting of the Strategic Planning Committee was called to assess, and now update.

An outline of that plan was promptly displayed as part of a series of colorful, smart–looking charts. To Daniel McCarthy, Riordan's CEO, these old poster board type props (a la Ross Perot) were still the most effective presentation tools, and were impressive illustrations of the progress his company had made this year, after two very tough years in the recession.

Strategic Plan

Riordan Industries manufactures thousands of specialty products for commercial and industrial use, but they divide along the major lines of electronics (43 percent of sales and 31 percent of profits), fluid controls and construction equipment (40 percent, 45 percent), and farm equipment (17 percent, 24 percent). During 1991, when the prospect for its businesses remained dim, the Strategic Planning Committee organized a comprehensive review of all of its major products, their markets, and all the inter–relationships among them. Fully accounting for joint as well as individual sales and profit contributions, the Committee established outlooks for various combinations of retained and disposed of product lines, thereby defining its businesses and, in the process, the company itself. From this it determined its overall strategic objectives and the action plan to bring it about. In doing so, it divested itself of about one–fourth of its fixed assets, and the related loss of about that, in its operating revenues.

This new "religion" produced many tangible benefits, such as state–of–the–art information and control systems, unparalleled customer service and satisfaction, and an average increase in its stock price of 7 percent per quarter over the last year and a half, to name a few. It also helped automate this review process, as evidenced by the bound, richly illustrated document lying in front of each of them. Barbara MacDonald, vice–president of information and quality assurance systems prepared the insightful report, and proceeded to discuss its findings.

First, she recommended that the company maintain its vigilance in identifying and dropping money–losing products and product lines. A few remaining "troubled" products were flagged for detailed review again this year. The group all agreed that this had produced real dividends in the past and should be continued.

Sources: Data and information based on various publications, including S&P Stock Reports, S&P Industry Surveys, and Value Line.

Second, of all the company's products and markets, the industrial and analytical instruments lines offer the greatest upside potential, in size and also in terms of profitability. Both market projections for these lines, and the company's own success in several new test measurement and control products, provide evidence of this assertion. But this was one of those good news, bad news situations, the bad news being that this was an area where the company was its weakest. The recommendation then to pursue joint ventures along these lines made a lot of sense.

A third major finding was to take actions, including an aggressive pursuance of new business, that would help moderate the highly volatile history of sales, earnings, and cash flow (see EXHIBIT 1). This too made a great deal of sense, for a number of obvious reasons. The gyrations depicted in the report's tables and graphs were really quite striking.

Perhaps the most troubling finding was a lack of unit growth in almost every area except, oddly enough, farm equipment. With continued pricing pressures in many of its markets, it would not be long before the company's financial results would be severely affected. Jack Welch, executive vice–president of finance, spoke up to confirm this. In fact, he added evidence of his own to confirm the difficulty of managing cash flows and, in the absence of some significant internally generated funds, the increasing reliance on debt to fund its operations. (The financial statement data on which this was based is summarized in EXHIBIT 2.)

A lively discussion on these and other points continued through the morning until the sight and smell of hot roast beef sandwiches broke the concentration. Mr. McCarthy called for the break and momentarily left the room.

Possible Business Ventures

The afternoon roundtable was highly unstructured, frequently bouncing from one topic to another, and between various related and sometimes unrelated solutions. One of the more far–reaching discussions centered on a possible merger with or acquisition of an existing instruments firm. This would thrust the company into its most promising business, flatten the learning curve in an industry in which it had not exactly excelled, and perhaps even moderate its volatile operating and financial performance.

These possibilities were debated at length, and by the end of the day, Jack Welch was volunteered to investigate, at least superficially for now, what the potential benefits would be of any of a number of possible business combinations. Although an acquisition was not likely in the near term, it was decided that if such a combination had real potential, the company could ease into a relationship with a joint venture as its first step.

Working with his treasurer, Jack Welch subsequently identified six firms in which Riordan might be interested. The specific subindustries these companies represented included laboratory analytical instruments (Firm A), measurement, display, and process control instruments (Firm B), measuring and controlling devices, n.e.c. (Firm C and E), electrical test and measurement instruments (Firm D), and laboratory apparatus and furniture (Firm F). Since volatility was a critical issue to any decision, Mr. Welch began by assembling market data (S&P 500 and T–bill rates of return in EXHIBIT 3), and quarterly accounting and market data on each of these companies (see EXHIBIT 4).

The plan of attack was to evaluate these six candidates initially in terms of relative variability in sales, earnings, cash flows and rates of return, both market and accounting measures (including returns on revenue, assets, and equity), and in particular, relative to Riordan's results. And since all of these companies had suffered similar fates in recent years, he thought that this, additionally, might produce insightful measures of relative managerial abilities.

Discussion Questions

1. Calculate the covariance between Riordan's market equity returns and the overall market, as measured by the S&P 500. Use the market variance to standardize this as a "beta" estimate. Develop the "characteristic line" between Riordan and the market, by regressing the equity rates of return. What do the regression statistics reveal about the quality of these beta estimates?

2. Calculate the covariance between Riordan's market equity returns and those of each of the six firms. Which of the six potential partners would help minimize Riordan's variability in market returns? What problems are there with this approach?

3. How can the relative variability of sales, earnings and cash flows be gauged between Riordan and possible partners?

4. How well do market returns track accounting returns on equity? Using accounting returns, how much of their variability is due to margin, to turnover, and to leverage?

5. Based on these analyses, which company should Riordan approach as a potential joint venture partner if the ultimate goal was to merge operations? Why?

6. Provide a summary illustration of how Riordan Industries would look financially, with and without such an acquisition.

7. What additional information would be useful for this analysis?

Exhibit 1
Quarterly Financial Data, 1988–1992
Riordan Industries, Inc.

($mm) Fiscal Year Ended August 31	Sales	Oper. Inc.	Earnings	Divid.	Deprec.	Assets	Equity	Price
1988	47.9	4.7	3.9	3.3	1.6	151.9	96.7	10.4
	43.5	4.3	(1.4)	1.6	1.6	161.3	93.7	12.3
	47.5	4.6	1.8	1.6	1.6	171.4	94.0	15.0
	45.2	4.4	5.8	0.0	1.6	182.0	99.8	14.3
1989	62.8	4.3	3.5	3.4	1.8	185.9	99.6	12.8
	57.6	4.0	(2.0)	1.8	1.8	189.8	95.8	14.8
	63.0	4.3	1.8	1.8	1.8	193.9	95.8	14.0
	60.6	4.2	3.9	0.0	1.8	198.0	99.7	13.8
1990	62.1	3.1	2.8	3.5	2.0	198.0	98.9	11.5
	55.7	2.8	1.3	1.8	2.0	198.0	98.4	11.4
	61.6	3.1	1.2	1.8	2.0	198.0	97.8	12.0
	61.9	3.1	(1.4)	0.0	2.0	198.0	96.5	8.8
1991	64.8	2.1	1.4	2.3	2.0	195.5	95.7	4.4
	59.1	1.9	0.2	1.1	2.0	192.9	94.7	7.4
	63.4	2.0	0.8	1.1	2.0	190.5	94.3	7.0
	56.3	1.8	(0.8)	0.0	2.0	188.0	93.6	7.1
1992	45.6	2.4	2.0	1.8	1.4	179.7	92.5	6.9
	43.1	2.3	(5.2)	0.6	1.4	171.8	86.7	6.0
	47.6	2.5	1.7	0.6	1.4	164.2	87.8	8.3
	47.4	2.5	1.7	0.0	1.4	157.0	89.5	7.8

Exhibit 2
Financial Statement Data
1988–1992

($mm) Year Ended August 31	1988	1989	1990	1991	1992
Operating Revenues	209	239	241	244	184
Operating Expenses	185	215	221	228	169
Depreciation	6	7	8	8	6
Interest Expense	3	6	7	7	6
Other Income	1	0	1	1	(2)
Income Taxes	36	4	2	0	1
Net Income	10	7	4	2	0
Cash	1	1	1	1	2
Other Current Assets	126	141	142	133	113
Long–Term Assets	55	56	55	54	42
Total Assets	182	198	198	188	157
Total Current Liabilities	60	46	51	41	37
Long–Term Debt	20	49	48	52	50
Other Long–Term Capital	2	3	3	3	2
Common Equity	100	100	97	92	64

Exhibit 3
Quarterly Rates of Return in the S&P 500 and T–Bills
1987–1992

	S&P 500	T–Bill		S&P 500	T–Bill		S&P 500	T–Bill
1987	21.3%	5.6%	1989	7.1%	8.8%	1991	14.5%	5.9%
	5.0	5.7		8.8	8.2		(0.2)	5.6
	6.6	6.3		10.7	7.7		5.3	5.3
	(22.5)	5.8		2.0	7.6		8.3	4.1
1988	5.7	5.7	1990	(3.0)	8.1	1992	(2.5)	4.1
	6.6	6.5		6.3	7.7		1.9	3.7
	0.3	7.2		(13.7)	7.4		3.2	3.0
	3.0	8.1		8.9	6.8		5.0	3.3

Exhibit 4
Financial Data

	Sales	Oper. Inc.	Earnings	Divid.	Deprec.	Assets	Equity	Price
			Firm A (FY 6/30)					
1988	16.1	3.8	2.7	0.0	0.4	73.5	58.6	28.0
	17.5	4.2	3.0	0.0	0.4	77.1	61.6	21.8
	18.0	4.3	3.1	0.0	0.4	81.0	64.6	30.6
	18.1	4.3	2.9	0.0	0.4	85.0	67.5	28.3
1989	17.3	3.7	2.9	0.0	0.4	88.3	72.5	23.8
	18.9	4.0	3.3	0.0	0.4	91.7	75.8	24.4
	19.5	4.2	3.4	0.0	0.4	95.3	79.2	18.6
	19.7	4.2	3.2	0.0	0.4	99.0	82.4	19.0
1990	18.8	3.7	3.3	0.0	0.5	100.7	84.4	22.9
	20.3	4.0	3.4	0.0	0.5	102.4	87.8	24.3
	20.5	4.0	3.4	0.0	0.5	104.2	91.2	22.1
	21.0	4.1	2.9	0.0	0.5	106.0	94.1	23.0
1991	20.6	4.4	3.1	0.0	0.5	106.7	86.8	17.5
	22.5	4.8	3.5	0.0	0.5	107.5	90.3	19.8
	23.3	4.9	3.8	0.0	0.5	108.2	94.1	27.0
	22.9	4.9	3.8	0.0	0.5	109.0	97.9	32.0
1992	21.5	4.6	3.1	0.0	0.5	111.7	88.4	28.4
	24.0	5.1	3.7	0.0	0.5	114.4	92.2	28.5
	25.1	5.4	3.9	0.0	0.5	117.2	96.0	31.0
	25.8	5.5	4.0	0.0	0.5	120.0	100.0	25.8
			Firm B (FY 12/31)					
1988	46.9	1.1	(0.5)	0.0	1.4	149.0	82.9	13.1
	54.4	1.3	0.4	0.0	1.4	146.9	83.3	12.0
	52.4	1.2	(0.7)	0.0	1.4	145.0	82.6	12.6
	54.3	1.3	(3.1)	0.0	1.4	143.0	79.5	11.9
1989	51.1	2.6	0.5	0.0	1.5	151.3	74.6	11.5
	57.9	3.0	(0.1)	0.0	1.5	160.0	74.5	11.5
	58.3	3.0	0.8	0.0	1.5	169.2	75.3	10.9
	57.9	3.0	2.3	0.0	1.5	179.0	77.6	13.3
1990	48.6	0.9	(2.0)	0.0	1.9	178.0	76.8	12.9
	63.9	1.2	2.2	0.0	1.9	177.0	79.0	12.3
	62.6	1.2	(1.9)	0.0	1.9	176.0	77.1	11.0
	62.9	1.2	(6.4)	0.0	1.9	175.0	70.7	7.8
1991	58.2	0.8	0.2	0.0	1.8	169.5	73.9	9.3
	61.3	0.8	0.1	0.0	1.8	164.2	73.9	10.4
	55.5	0.8	(2.3)	0.0	1.8	159.0	71.6	9.0
	62.0	0.7	(20.4)	0.0	1.8	154.0	51.2	7.0
1992	53.4	0.9	0.3	0.0	1.9	156.7	47.1	7.8
	56.4	1.0	0.3	0.0	1.9	159.4	47.4	8.8
	64.7	1.1	0.6	0.0	1.9	162.2	48.0	7.6
	56.8	1.0	0.5	0.0	1.9	165.0	48.5	10.1

Exhibit 4 (cont.)

	Sales	Oper. Inc.	Earnings	Divid.	Deprec.	Assets	Equity	Price
				Firm C (FY 12/31)				
1988	26.4	1.5	0.5	0.2	0.8	81.8	34.3	13.0
	27.8	1.6	0.4	0.2	0.8	83.3	34.5	14.9
	25.1	1.4	0.4	0.2	0.8	84.8	34.7	12.3
	32.2	1.8	1.2	0.2	0.8	86.3	35.8	11.5
1989	26.6	1.9	0.6	0.2	0.8	85.9	35.9	11.3
	27.8	2.0	0.5	0.2	0.8	85.6	36.2	13.3
	25.2	1.8	0.5	0.2	0.8	85.2	36.6	10.5
	31.8	2.3	1.6	0.2	0.8	84.9	38.0	9.6
1990	26.4	2.0	0.6	0.2	0.9	87.9	36.7	8.3
	30.6	2.3	0.9	0.2	0.9	91.1	37.4	9.9
	29.1	2.2	0.9	0.2	0.9	94.3	38.1	9.3
	35.2	2.7	1.9	0.2	0.9	97.7	39.8	8.0
1991	32.2	2.7	1.2	0.2	0.9	96.7	44.8	9.9
	31.1	2.6	0.6	0.2	0.9	95.7	45.2	12.5
	26.4	2.2	0.8	0.2	0.9	94.8	45.8	12.6
	36.7	3.1	2.7	0.2	0.9	93.8	48.2	9.3
1992	28.5	1.9	0.8	0.2	1.0	94.1	48.5	12.1
	29.2	1.9	0.6	0.2	1.0	94.4	49.0	10.3
	26.6	1.7	0.5	0.2	1.0	94.7	49.3	9.6
	32.0	2.1	1.8	0.2	1.0	95.0	50.8	10.0
				Firm D (FY 6/30)				
1988	28.4	3.1	1.6	0.0	0.9	119.7	88.7	21.5
	27.0	2.9	1.6	0.0	0.9	124.6	90.4	13.6
	28.2	3.1	1.6	0.0	0.9	129.7	92.0	18.0
	29.3	3.2	3.9	0.0	0.9	135.0	95.9	18.3
1989	42.1	4.6	1.6	0.0	1.6	141.1	99.1	13.1
	40.1	4.4	1.6	0.0	1.6	147.4	100.6	11.9
	42.4	4.6	2.1	0.0	1.6	154.1	102.7	11.8
	40.9	4.5	6.5	0.0	1.6	161.0	109.2	12.1
1990	43.2	3.3	2.5	0.0	2.2	165.3	113.5	12.3
	40.2	3.1	2.5	0.0	2.2	169.8	116.1	8.8
	41.6	3.2	2.2	0.0	2.2	174.3	118.2	8.1
	42.9	3.3	2.2	0.0	2.2	179.0	120.4	11.4
1991	36.1	1.2	0.4	0.0	2.3	183.6	122.5	7.6
	34.8	1.2	0.4	0.0	2.3	188.3	122.8	7.9
	36.6	1.2	0.4	0.0	2.3	193.1	123.2	11.3
	40.9	1.4	1.3	0.0	2.3	198.0	124.5	12.3
1992	41.0	(1.4)	0.4	0.0	2.7	195.5	113.6	11.5
	39.6	(1.4)	0.4	0.0	2.7	192.9	113.9	9.4
	42.7	(1.5)	(2.4)	0.0	2.7	190.5	111.5	11.3
	32.7	(1.1)	(14.9)	0.0	2.7	188.0	96.6	8.9

Exhibit 4 (cont.)

	Sales	Oper. Inc.	Earnings	Divid.	Deprec.	Assets	Equity	Price
Firm E (FY 9/30)								
1988	29.8	3.3	2.4	0.3	1.0	101.6	53.4	15.8
	29.8	3.3	1.9	0.3	1.0	105.2	55.0	21.9
	29.1	3.2	1.4	0.3	1.0	109.0	56.1	24.1
	40.3	4.5	3.4	0.3	1.0	113.0	59.2	19.5
1989	34.1	4.1	2.6	0.3	1.1	116.1	61.4	19.4
	35.9	4.3	2.6	0.3	1.1	119.3	63.7	19.9
	35.0	4.2	1.7	0.3	1.1	122.6	65.0	20.0
	47.6	5.8	4.2	0.3	1.1	126.0	68.9	21.6
1990	36.2	2.9	2.8	0.5	1.4	126.2	71.7	22.3
	38.1	3.0	2.1	0.5	1.4	126.5	73.3	23.9
	38.3	3.1	1.4	0.5	1.4	126.7	74.2	24.1
	47.6	3.8	2.1	0.5	1.4	127.0	75.9	19.6
1991	38.5	4.2	2.2	0.4	1.5	129.2	76.2	15.5
	34.7	3.8	1.6	0.4	1.5	131.4	77.3	18.1
	32.9	3.6	1.4	0.4	1.5	133.7	78.3	20.0
	51.8	5.7	4.9	0.4	1.5	136.0	82.7	22.8
1992	32.4	1.6	0.8	0.5	1.5	138.2	80.9	25.8
	39.9	2.0	1.4	0.5	1.5	140.4	81.8	27.4
	38.8	1.9	0.7	0.5	1.5	142.7	82.0	28.1
	49.9	2.5	2.0	0.5	1.5	145.0	83.4	24.0
Firm F (FY 7/31)								
1988	13.0	2.1	1.0	0.1	0.6	77.5	70.0	8.9
	13.4	2.2	1.6	0.1	0.6	77.0	71.5	9.5
	13.6	2.2	2.3	0.2	0.6	76.5	73.7	12.0
	13.4	2.2	2.4	0.2	0.6	76.0	75.9	13.9
1989	13.3	1.8	0.6	0.2	0.7	77.2	64.9	13.5
	14.9	2.0	0.8	0.2	0.7	78.5	65.4	11.3
	14.9	2.0	2.4	0.2	0.7	79.7	67.5	11.9
	14.2	1.9	2.9	0.2	0.7	81.0	70.2	11.0
1990	14.7	1.2	0.8	0.3	0.8	80.0	71.1	10.5
	14.5	1.2	1.1	0.3	0.8	79.0	71.9	9.4
	15.1	1.2	1.4	0.3	0.8	78.0	73.0	9.0
	14.5	1.2	1.4	0.3	0.8	77.0	74.0	9.1
1991	14.8	1.0	0.6	0.3	0.7	79.6	64.6	8.0
	14.7	1.0	1.1	0.3	0.7	82.3	65.4	8.3
	14.8	1.0	1.0	0.3	0.7	85.1	66.1	9.8
	15.4	1.0	0.9	0.3	0.7	88.0	66.7	7.9
1992	17.3	0.0	0.1	0.3	1.6	92.6	63.7	9.3
	25.4	0.0	0.5	0.0	1.6	97.5	64.2	8.9
	24.2	0.0	(1.3)	0.6	1.6	102.6	62.3	6.8
	20.9	0.0	(2.0)	0.0	1.6	108.0	60.4	5.6

Part II
Capital Additions

Case 5
Fystrom Chemical Company, Inc.

It seemed amazing. This one project was larger than the company's entire capital budget from just a few years ago. What Alan Gamble, the director of capital projects, was referring to was a proposal from the company's Strategic Planning Committee for a new plant in Monterrey. Apparently, the company was serious about venturing into foreign–based production facilities. And this was, by far, the technologically most sophisticated facility the company had even considered—and in Mexico, no less.

Given the scope of this project, and the size and number of other capital requests this year, it seemed like a good time to formalize and systematize the analyses and reports on proposed capital additions. This was alluded to in the Capital Projects Department's 1992 goals, and was mentioned by the Executive Committee last year in the siting decision of the R&D facility.

Capital Budget

In 1991, Fystrom Chemical Company's capital budget was over $90 million, and was expected to top $100 million this year for the first time in its history. Even as a leading maker of bromine and brominated chemicals, this specialty chemical producer has relatively small–scale facilities, especially relative to chemical companies in general. But the continued growth of the company's markets necessitates an ever–growing plant expansion and modernization program, estimated to be as much as 25 percent per year for the next three to four years. The proposed Monterrey facility is expected to cost almost $30 million, and this is probably 20–30 percent less than a comparable plant constructed in the U.S. The alternative being considered to the Mexico project is a $15 million modification to the company's Crayco plant in Tennessee. Other projects that have been proposed include a major addition to its facility in Arkansas, which produces styrene and polystyrene resins; the acquisition of a custom chemical manufacturer, also in Arkansas; a joint venture with a British company which produces fuel additives; and various production and warehouse upgrades in a number of smaller plants in Florida, Georgia, and Tennessee.

The advisability, timing, and priority of each of these various projects is of utmost concern to the Executive Committee. Thus, in addition to analyzing the basic economics of these decisions, the Capital Projects Department is expected to provide reports that are more uniform in nature, and further, that contain the kind of information the Committee can use to establish priorities and to determine what size the capital budget should be in each of the next several years.

The analysis and report on the proposed Monterrey plant, or as an alternative, the rebuilt Crayco plant, is the perfect opportunity to develop this system of presentation. And to facilitate this, Alan Gamble

Sources: Data and information based on various publications, including S&P Stock Reports and S&P Industry Surveys.

decided to assemble a team of Steve Hysel, Sandy Steiner, and Charles Rayburn, and their respective staffs. Hysel is the chief engineer of these projects. Ms. Steiner is the company's consulting specialist in production and operations management. And Charles Rayburn is Fystrom's treasurer. Approximately $350,000 is being allotted to this function this year, and this will run close to half a million dollars next year. About half of this task force's time and effort will be spent on the Monterrey/Crayco project, and the rest on other capital projects and issues. Other cost considerations are detailed in the individual proposals.

Fystrom Chemical Company

Briefly, Fystrom Chemical Company is a producer of bromine, its derivatives, and furfural for use in fire control chemicals. It also produces agricultural fumigants, biocides and pesticide intermediates, and a variety of specialized industrial chemicals. The company is headquartered in a small town in southern Ohio, operates numerous production and warehouse facilities in several southern states, research and development labs in Georgia and Tennessee, and limited distribution operations in France, Germany, and Italy. It has grown from $170 million in sales in 1982, to over $1.3 billion in 1991. Although half of total sales are bromine chemicals, Fystrom has expanded into industrial and recreational water treatment chemicals, clear fluids used in oil and gas production, agricultural specialties, and intermediate chemicals for pharmaceuticals, photographic papers, dyes, and rubber compounds. As a result of this expansion, earnings have doubled in the last four years, and its stock price has tripled. Long–term debt is no more than a fourth of total capital, and cash flows have remained strong. All in all, the company has managed its diversification well, in addition to growing its core business in bromine products at double–digit rates.

The possible expansion into Mexico represents significant potential for the company, beyond the benefits of this one facility. But risks abound as well. Thus, it will be important to take a more complete view of this particular capital addition proposal than it might otherwise.

Monterrey Project

With the explosion of the "maquiladora" plants along the U.S.–Mexican border in the last decade, Fystrom gave a serious look to the possibility of a Mexican–based production facility a few years ago. The eight–to–one U.S.–Mexican wage differential in the chemical industry made it a particularly attractive proposition, but Mexico still had significant restrictions on foreign investment and with the political risk, it just didn't seem worth the effort. Now, however, President Carlos Salinas de Gortari is firmly in charge of Mexico's modernization and economic development, the North American Free Trade Agreement has been ratified, and both the U.S. and Mexican economies are once again expanding. The significance of these factors are that political risk is reduced (e.g., agreements that control wages and prices now hold), investment restrictions are being lifted, and markets are growing. A particular sticking point in the past was the 40 percent limit on foreign ownership of secondary (non–basic) chemical producers. A major part of the Free Trade Agreement is the opening up of the Mexican chemical industry to outsiders. The country will remove restrictions on private investment in 14 of the 19 so–called primary chemicals and all restrictions on foreign investment in the 66 secondary chemical products.

Unlike the "maquiladora" plants where U.S.–made parts are trucked across the border, assembled by low–skill, low–wage Mexican workers, and then shipped back to markets in the U.S., the Monterrey Project would represent a development of the chemical industry in Mexico, both in terms of inputs and outputs. And the impressive 87 percent Mexican literacy rate makes the investment in human capital as productive as physical capital investments.

Specifically, Fystrom is considering the construction of a $28.75 million facility 30 miles outside of Monterrey which would produce furfural ($C_5H_4O_2$) and furfural–based derivatives used to make foundry resins, urethanes and chemical intermediates, and refining solvents. Sales are estimated to be $48.6 million in the first year after completion of the plant, and should grow by 10 percent per year. Profit margin is expected to be around 6 percent in the first year of operation, but with such a capital–intensive operation, it should increase every year thereafter. Additional details of the Monterrey Project are provided in EXHIBIT 1.

Crayco Plant Modification

As an alternative to the Mexican expansion, the company could modify an existing facility it already owns in Tennessee. The Crayco Plant was idled a few years ago and has since been salvaged. It was not well suited for the type of plant expansions the company invested in recently, but it could be adaptable for the furfural operation. Currently, it consists of a modest–sized site with a series of industrial buildings, which have been gutted. If not used for this purpose, it probably would be held for some future company activity and leased out on a net, net, net basis for $60,000 per year.

The estimated cost of adapting the Crayco site to a furfural plant is $15 million. In addition to this lower capital cost, construction could begin as early as January, 1993. The plant could be generating $45 million in sales by 1995, but they are expected to grow by only 7 percent per year. Operating leverage would be somewhat lower with the U.S. plant, but it could generate around a 6 percent initial margin as well. The company typically uses a 12 percent cost of capital figure to discount cash flows, and a 10–year plant operating period as an investment horizon. Additional details on the Crayco Plant modification are contained in EXHIBIT 2.

The Capital Projects Department usually conducts an economic evaluation of a proposed project first, and then, if it seems feasible, investigates other dimensions to the problem, further refines the estimates, and then reports out. For most projects, the department's reports go back to the Strategic Planning Committee, which in turn evaluates them and forwards recommendations to the Executive Committee. Alan Gamble is a member of the Strategic Planning Committee but is not one of the Executive Committee members.

Discussion Questions

1. What economic concepts should be applied in making capital addition decisions?

2. Calculate the cash flows associated with the Monterrey Project. Compare these to those of the Crayco Plant Modification.

3. What are proper investment criteria? Calculate these and illustrate the differences between the two projects.

4. Illustrate the differences in operating leverage.

5. How should risk be addressed in these proposals?

6. What would be your recommendation between these two mutually exclusive projects, and why? Illustrate.

7. Provide examples of what a uniform report would look like for presentation to the Strategic Planning and Executive Committee.

8. What additional information would be useful for the analysis?

Exhibit 1
Monterrey Project
Assumptions[*]

Land Acquisition	$1.75 million in 1993
Development, Construction	$13.0 million in 1994, $8.0 million in 1995
	Construction interest @8% per annum
Equipment	$6.0 million in 1996
Net Working Capital	$100,000 in 1996 plus 25% of Sales
Sales	$48.6 million in 1997, increasing by 10%/yr. for 10 years
Cost of Goods Sold	65% of Sales
Fixed Expense	$11.5 million in 1997, increasing by 5%/yr.
Depreciation	Building 31.5 yrs., Equipment 7 yrs. ACRS
Income Taxes	23%
Salvage Values	Building 20% of cost, Equipment 0%

[*]All amounts in nominal U.S. dollars.

Exhibit 2
Crayco Plant Modification
Assumptions[*]

Land Acquisition	Company owns site
Development, Construction	$15.0 million in 1993
	Construction interest @8% per annum
Equipment	$6.0 million in 1994
Net Working Capital	$100,000 in 1994 plus 25% of Sales
Sales	$45.0 million in 1995, increasing by 7%/yr. for 10 years
Cost of Goods Sold	80% of Sales
Fixed Expense	$4.0 million in 1995, increasing by 5%/yr.
Depreciation	Building 31.5 yrs., Equipment 7 yrs. ACRS
Income Taxes	23%
Salvage Values	Building 20% of cost, Equipment 0%

[*]All amounts in nominal U.S. dollars.

Case 6
Mosher Pumps, Inc.

In the small industrial pump business, Mosher Pumps have been the industry standard for over 20 years. The company's engineers have literally revolutionized the industry by developing new concepts and innovations designed to meet the market's ever–changing and growing requirements. The company currently manufactures more than 150 different models, yet maintains flexibility for itself and its customers with a unique system of interchangeable parts, allowing conversion from one model to another within the same frame size in minutes. This modular flexibility means a more dependable pump because of uniformity of parts and quality control during manufacture. It also means faster delivery and service. And to the Mosher Pumps distributors, this modular approach means lower cost pump and parts inventory.

Quality and service have been the watchwords at Mosher Pumps since its inception, and President Jerry Mosher, an engineer and also head of research and development, will tell you that this, too, is by design. Long before it became popular in other business organizations, R & D at Mosher Pumps was an integrated, interdisciplinary function of engineers, market researchers, financial analysts, and customer representatives. And the extensive two–way communication and exchange of information between the company and its customers is like nothing else in this or other similar industries. Jerry Mosher is as proud of the many awards and recognitions his company has received for service as he is in the long list of technical excellence awards the company has accumulated, dating back to 1976.

Mosher Pumps designs and manufactures a complete line of small, high pressure pumps and accessories for industrial usage in a wide range of industries. Common applications include pressure cleaning, salt water injecting, wet sandblasting, hydrostatic testing, and many others. These products are sold and serviced in 42 states, throughout Canada, in 40 countries worldwide, and extensively in South America, Europe, and now Asia.

Retail Market

A couple of months ago Karen Black, the head of customer research, circulated a report among senior management indicating that there was significant potential for the company's technology in the retail market. She had been studying industry trends for many years and had concluded that the retail market for heavy–duty paint sprayers, roller painters, and surface preparation tools such as pressure washers, paint strippers, and heat guns was ready to take off. Jerry Mosher knew of the R & D work that had been done in these product areas the last few years and was confident the company could bring a high quality line of products to market within a year, if the market was indeed ready for them. Vice–president of sales, Ed O'Keefe, had investigated retail channels for such products and was particularly optimistic because of the potential size of this market. The only remaining area to be considered was, of course, the financial feasibility of the venture. This was the purview of Joseph Hanifl, senior vice–president of finance.

Sources: Company Reports.

Project Specifics

In their preliminary work, Mr. Hanifl's staff identified two principal areas of uncertainty with the proposed venture—the size of the market, and the effectiveness with which the company could compete in the retail market. In particular, the actual equipment and processes would be very different in design and scale depending on market size, with the order of magnitude being 3 to 1 from largest to smallest market scenarios. The second factor, competitiveness, was a real unknown since it could not be researched. But the staff did model "high" and "low" degrees of competitiveness in order to determine if this would affect the size question. Their sales estimates for the company's products in three different potential market sizes and with two degrees of competitiveness are provided in EXHIBIT 1.

In the base case, cost of goods sold was assumed to be 70 percent of sales, and operating expenses were $150,000, $250,000, and $400,000 per year for the small, medium, and large facilities, respectively. Start–up costs were assumed to be $100,000, $200,000 and $300,000 in each of the three scales, but in 1993 only. All cases assumed a $1,000,000 one–time expenditure in 1994 to develop a major introduction and promotion of the product line. Equipment cost should be depreciated with the modified ACRS percentages for 7-year property. The income tax rate for study purposes is 40 percent, and the cost of capital is 12 percent. At the end of five years, the equipment should have a market value of approximately one–third of its original cost. Finally, net working capital needs are assumed to be 10 percent of the following year's sales. The Net Present Value of this base case (Medium High) was $2.623 million with a "high" degree of competitiveness, producing a 16.8 percent Internal Rate of Return.

Alternatives and Risk Analysis

When the parties met to discuss the alternatives, it was quite clear that Mr. O'Keefe was very optimistic about the size of the market. It was obvious to him that the large facility would produce the greatest net present value. Mr. Hanifl's conservatism dominated his thoughts, and it was equally obvious to him that building the small facility was the only prudent action to take. Even under the "low" competitiveness scenario, it produced a return equal to the company's cost of capital. Mr. Mosher was thinking in terms of the consequences of making the wrong decision and arrived at the decision to build the medium–sized facility.

This seemed like a classic case of the blind men and the elephant. What was needed here was some perspective. He decided to order a full–blown simulation—at least this way all alternatives could be considered, and the relationships between and among the variables could be "seen" through the results.

As they discussed some of the key assumptions, it was decided that in addition to the different market sizes and competitiveness scenarios, the estimating error in the initial sales figure (1993 estimates), the cost of goods sold percentage, and operating expense estimates should be explicitly considered for possible variations from "expected." Subsequent work produced the alternative values for these key assumptions, and the subjective probabilities of each occurring, which are provided in EXHIBIT 2.

The company was proud of its track record in the industrial pump business, with hardly a single misstep in its 20–year history. It was also proud of its ability to know its markets and its customers. But this time the company would be dealing with the retail market, where its knowledge of the customers and the company's competitors was purely from secondary sources. With this thought, Mr. Mosher turned to his staff and said, "We'll figure this thing out—we'll get it right." Jerry Mosher never settled for anything less.

Discussion Questions

1. What are the NPVs and IRRs with each of the alternatives? What choice do they suggest? Why?

2. What scale facility would Mr. O'Keefe's optimistic outlook suggest? Mr. Hanifl's conservation position? If Mr. O'Keefe's preferences were termed the maximax decision criteria and Mr. Hanifl's choice the maximin decision criteria, what is the choice under minimax (regret) decision criteria (opportunity cost of wrong decision)?

3. If the "high" and "low" competitiveness scenarios had equal chances of occurring (probabilities unknown), what scale facility should be built? What scale facility should be built if the probabilities for "high" and "low" are .40 and .60, respectively?

4. Conduct a simulation with the data provided in Exhibit 2. What do the process and the results reveal?

5. What other options could be considered in making this decision?

6. What additional information would be useful for this analysis?

Exhibit 1
Equipment Cost and Estimated Sales Growth
1992–1997

	Equipment Cost*		Sales*				
	1992		**1993**	**1994**	**1995**	**1996**	**1997**
Small:	8,250	High	7,000	8,050	10,063	13,081	17,660
		Low	6,364	7,318	9,148	11,892	16,054
Medium:	15,000	High	14,000	16,100	20,125	26,163	35,319
		Low	10,000	11,500	14,375	18,688	25,228
Large:	23,000	High	22,000	25,300	31,625	41,113	55,502
		Low	13,750	15,813	19,766	25,695	34,689

*In thousands of dollars.

Exhibit 2
Key Input Assumptions

	Alternative	Probability
Initial (1993) Sales Estimate	1.10 x	.05
	1.05 x	.15
	1.00 x	.60
	.95 x	.15
	.90 x	.05
Cost of Goods Sold Proportion	.675	.15
	.70	.50
	.725	.20
	.75	.15
Operating Expenses	.75 x	.15
	1.0 x	.55
	1.5 x	.30

Case 7
Tenneson Property Investors, Inc.

Making money in income–producing real estate these days is a real art. Even without the excesses of the late 1980s, this torpid economy of the 1990s humbles the best of asset managers. Thus, as real estate investment trusts go, Tenneson Property Investors, Inc., can consider itself fortunate to be generating positive returns on its assets, no matter how moderate they may seem in historical perspective. But as a specialist in troubled properties, it truly has a competitive advantage. As some indication of Tenneson Property's performance in recent years, EXHIBIT 1 tells the tale of decline in a tough market (after a number of highly profitable years), and then the first hope of a rebound with the 1992 results. From the investor's perspective, this hope is more of an expectation, since there has been a real loss of return over this period, given opportunity costs.

In fact, investors are expecting even more active management of the trust's portfolio in the years ahead in order to justify their continued investment. Of course, an improving economy would help profitability of existing assets tremendously. And, as discussed in its annual report, the reallocation of investments by type and geographical market should add significantly to future earnings. But investors want more. Specifically, they think this trust's management is especially adept at identifying bargains in the current real estate market, in distressed properties. They see additional profit potential in the successful rehabilitation of such properties. This was clearly communicated to management at their recent annual shareholders meeting. Their "fear" of the last couple of years has now been replaced with "greed."

Nature of Current Investments

Tenneson Property Investors began as a mortgage trust in the early 1970s, but gradually shifted to equity investments as opportunities and circumstances (e.g., defaults on mortgages held) permitted. As of November 1992, over 90 percent of the trust's assets were in equity investments. As an operating principle, Tenneson purchases struggling properties with potential for significant appreciation, if properly managed or reoriented. Properties must produce sufficient cash to at least break even, and geographical location is limited to predetermined target areas, where the economy has a solid industrial base and a track record of responsible local government. EXHIBIT 2 gives a state and regional breakdown of Tenneson's current portfolio.

Portfolio allocations by property type are reviewed quarterly to meet risk–return goals set out in its one– and three–year business plans. In terms of total number of properties, apartment complexes make up the largest component, almost 40 percent, and enjoy the highest occupancy levels. Shopping centers

Sources: Data and information based on various publications, including S&P Stock Reports and Survey of Current Business.

and office buildings are turned over more often, to capitalize on gains from rehabing and re–leasing of these properties. Each category tends to vary, but generally both are within 20–25 percent of total holdings. Finally, industrial properties are largely "buy–and–hold" investments and usually run around 15 percent. Details of Tenneson's portfolio as of the end of 1992 are provided in EXHIBIT 3.

Recent Management Actions

As part of the trust's on–going management activities, several properties have been refinanced (re–leveraged) recently, and a couple major interests have been sold. Excess cash has risen to $15 million as a result, and could be up to $20 million in the next few months. As such, the search for new properties has accelerated somewhat, including a recent visit to the Resolution Trust Corporation (RTC). Although the government's savings and loan bailout agency has long since had its assets cherry–picked, Tenneson does make periodic contact, because properties, and particularly circumstances, do change.

Tenneson's acquisitions and dispositions director is Janice De Laney, a very skillful negotiator with a good eye for value. In preparation for her visit to the RTC, she asked Robert Raasch, her research assistant, to update the state of the state economies in which Tenneson currently has interests. An excerpt from his report is reproduced in EXHIBIT 4. Further breakdown by metro area was provided as well, but it is not shown here. In short, the areas where real estate demand has begun to catch up with supply is in Knoxville and Nashville, Tennessee, and in Green Bay and Milwaukee, Wisconsin.

Two properties which looked interesting in this context were a 400–acre planned residential community about 35 miles north of Milwaukee with apartment complexes that were a little more than half full, and a apartment building in downtown Knoxville that has experienced high tenant turnover since its inception. The first property includes numerous single–family home sites undeveloped, and a golf course being completed by another developer under the sponsorship of present landowners. Phase I is only about 60 percent completed, although the apartment buildings have all been built. A Phase II resort–inn never got off the drawing board. The second potential investment is a building in a downtown location which has small units. If a new convention center currently being discussed becomes a reality, the property could be converted to a suite hotel and thrive from its proximity to the center.

Ms. De Laney visited both properties recently and discussed the development potential of each with associates the trust has worked with before. Details of her preliminary investigation and estimates for the two properties are provided here.

Apartments/Golf Resort–Inn Property

This partially completed development north of Milwaukee would require participation with a home builder, since the RTC wants to market the whole property in one sale, and the trust has no interest in the home sites. The current golf course developer may be willing to invest, but if not, the assumption is that another partner could be found. The apartment complex is made up of six 40–unit buildings that are about 60 percent occupied at this point. Preliminary market research suggests that a 90 percent occupancy rate is feasible in two years with proper management and marketing. The average monthly rent of $650 per unit is comparable to that of competing properties in the area, and operating expenses should be around 40 percent of revenues. Ms. De Laney believes that for this part of a bid, $11–$12 million is likely to be accepted by the RTC. Tenneson could make either an all–equity investment, or finance up to 80 percent of the purchase price. Other details and assumptions are given in EXHIBIT 5.

One exciting possibility for this property is the conversion to a resort/convention facility. Because of the orientation of the six buildings and the available land between them, a golf resort/inn type use of the real estate is feasible. In three years, the development should be far enough along to allow for this possibility, and for as little as $4–$5 million (all equity) for a convention–meeting facility and some modifications to the units. Such properties rarely achieve better than a 60 percent occupancy, and then only with aggressive promotion packages. Under this scenario, rooms would likely yield no more than $85–$100 per night on average, and require about 60 percent in operating expenses to manage. Approximately $300,000 annually in other revenues would be typical of a facility such as this. These estimates, in nominal dollars three years from now, are only averages, and cash flows could vary by 25 percent (the standard deviation). Again, this is only a possibility, but a realistic one.

Apartments/Hotel Suites Property

The second property offers a similar opportunity. Located in downtown Knoxville, this six–year old, 180–unit building is 80 percent occupied. Its studio apartments rent for $450 per month and appeal mostly to short–term tenants, so a 20 percent vacancy rate isn't bad. But this could be improved, if only slightly, to 15 percent with better tenant selection. And a 35 percent operating expense ratio is attainable for this property, if thoughtfully managed. Ms. De Laney believes the RTC would settle for about $6 million for this asset, due to a profound lack of interest by buyers. Again, this investment could be an all–equity deal or be financed with an 80 percent LTV (loan–to–value) mortgage. Like the other property, the expected sale price of this building three years from now would be a function of the achieved escalation in rents. The details on this potential project are provided in EXHIBIT 6.

Given the size, configuration, and unique location of this building, a suite–type hotel is a possibility for its future use, but only if demand for hotel rooms in the downtown area were to increase. A major development which would assuredly create this demand is a new convention center being proposed two blocks from the subject property. Unfortunately, this is far from a done deal at present, and could ultimately be rejected by the voters because of concerns over the additional tax burden. But if it were approved, a $5 million investment in renovation and conversion in three years would be needed to produce whatever incremental cash flows the property could generate as a hotel. Although an estimate of these cash flows is unknown at this time, the estimate itself is likely to be subject to a standard deviation of 25 percent, as was the case with the other property.

Either property is a real gamble, if the basis for the decision to purchase them is on these potential converted uses. Yet these possibilities should not be ignored. The question is, how should these potential uses be valued, in decisions that have to be made now.

Discussion Questions

1. Based on the preliminary data for the two properties, do either or both investments meet the stated financial objectives for the trust's investments?

2. What could be done to improve the profitability of each of these investments? Be specific.

3. Consider the sources of risk with each of these investments. How would you evaluate the risk–return trade–off with these two properties?

4. If you considered the joint venture with the developer of the golf community as an option for the resort–inn three years hence, how would that affect the decision to invest? A reference table is provided in EXHIBIT 7. Likewise, if the investment in the apartment building were construed as a call option in the hotel suites conversion project, what effect would this have?

5. Illustrate the upside and downside of these investments in the call option framework.

6. What portfolio considerations, specifically, should enter into the decision to acquire either or both of these properties for the real estate investment trust?

7. What additional information would be useful for this analysis?

Exhibit 1
Financial Performance of the Trust
1987–1992

	1987	1988	1989	1990	1991	1992
Net Income/Revenues	9.9%	12.7%	7.7%	6.2%	6.2%	6.9%
Earnings plus Depr./Assets	8.9%	10.4%	7.0%	5.5%	5.5%	6.2%
Earnings per Share	$1.64	1.64	0.83	0.66	0.66	0.99
Dividends per Share	$1.60	1.60	1.36	1.04	0.80	0.89
Average Market Price	$17.1	18.9	15.1	9.8	9.7	11.7

Exhibit 2
Geographical Distribution of Current Investments
1992

West		South		Midwest		East	
Arizona	5%	Florida	18%	Illinois	14%	Maryland	11%
California	11%	Louisiana	6%	Michigan	12%	New Jersey	7%
		Tennessee	4%	Ohio	6%		
		Other So.	1%	Wisconsin	5%		
	16%		29%		37%		18%

Exhibit 3
Distribution of Current Investments by Type
1992

Property Type	Percentage of Portfolio	Total Space	Occupancy
Apartments	39%	1,752 units	95%
Shopping Centers	24%	705,600 sq. ft.	84%
Office Buildings	22%	556,400 sq. ft.	87%
Industrial	15%	1,109,700 sq. ft.	76%
	100%		

Exhibit 4
Income Growth
Strength of Recovery from the Recession
Annualized Rates from Trough of 1st Qtr., 1992*

Of the 10 Fastest Growing States in the Recovery, Tenneson has properties in:			Of the 10 Slowest Growing States in the Recovery, Tenneson has properties in:		
No. 3	Tennessee	6.5%	No. 2	Florida	2.0%
No. 9	Wisconsin	5.9%	No. 5	Maryland	3.5%
			No. 8	California	3.8%
			No. 10	New Jersey	3.8%

U.S. Average 4.4%

* Just as a reminder, the difference between 3% and 2% is not 1%, it's 50%. It takes 50% more labor, 50% more capital, etc., to grow at 3% than 2%.

Exhibit 5
Golf Community Joint Venture
Milwaukee, Wisconsin

Purchase Price	$11–12 million
Possible Financing	80% LTV at 9%, 30 years, with monthly payments
Building/Land Values	70%/30%
Rents	$650/mo./unit, escalating at 3% per year
Vacancy Rate	30% first year, 20% second year, 10% thereafter
Operating Expense Ratio	30% of Effect. Gross Inc., escal. at 5% per year
Sales Price in 3 Years	Based on multiple of Gross Potential Income
Sales Commission	6%
Upgrade at the End of 3 Years	$4-5 million
Occupancy	60%
Room Rate	$85–100
Operating Expenses	60%
Cost of Capital	15%

Exhibit 6
Apartment Building/Hotel Suites Project
Knoxville, Tennessee

Purchase Price	$6 million
Possible Financing	80% LTV at 9%, 30 years, with monthly payments
Building/Land Values	90%/10%
Rents	$500/mo./unit, escalating at 2% per year
Vacancy Rate	15%
Operating Expense Ratio	35% of Effect. Gross Inc., escal. at 5% per year
Sales Price in 3 Years	Based on multiple of Gross Potential Income
Sales Commission	6%
Upgrade at the End of 3 Years	$5 million
Annual Cash Flow	unknown
Cost of Capital	15%

Exhibit 7
Call Option Values, Percent of Share Price

Share Price/ Exercise Price	Standard Deviation × Square Root of Time						
	.25	.35	.40	.45	.50	.55	.60
.80	2.8%	6.2%	8.0%	9.9%	11.8%	13.8%	15.8%
.82	3.3	6.8	8.7	10.6	12.6	14.6	16.6
.84	3.9	7.5	9.4	11.4	13.4	15.4	17.4
.86	4.5	8.2	10.2	12.2	14.2	16.1	18.1
.88	5.2	9.0	11.0	12.9	14.9	16.9	18.9
.90	5.9	9.8	11.7	13.7	15.7	17.7	19.7
.92	6.6	10.6	12.5	14.5	16.5	18.5	20.5
.94	7.4	11.4	13.4	15.3	17.3	19.3	21.3
.96	8.2	12.2	14.2	16.2	18.1	20.1	22.0
.98	9.1	13.0	15.0	17.0	18.9	20.9	22.8
1.00	9.9	13.9	15.9	17.8	19.7	21.7	23.6
1.02	10.9	14.8	16.7	18.6	20.5	22.4	24.3
1.04	11.8	15.6	17.5	19.4	21.3	23.2	25.1
1.06	12.8	16.5	18.4	20.3	22.1	24.0	25.8
1.08	13.7	17.4	19.2	21.1	22.9	24.8	26.6
1.10	14.7	18.3	20.1	21.9	23.7	25.5	27.3
1.12	15.7	19.2	20.9	22.7	24.5	26.3	28.1
1.14	16.7	20.1	21.8	23.5	25.3	27.0	28.8
1.16	17.7	21.0	22.6	24.3	26.1	27.8	29.5
1.18	18.7	21.9	23.5	25.1	26.8	28.5	30.2
1.20	19.8	22.7	24.3	25.9	27.6	29.2	30.9
1.25	22.3	24.9	26.4	27.9	29.5	31.0	32.6
1.30	24.7	27.1	28.4	29.8	31.3	32.8	34.3
1.35	27.1	29.2	30.4	31.7	33.1	34.5	35.9
1.40	29.4	31.2	32.3	33.5	34.8	36.1	37.5
1.45	31.7	33.2	34.2	35.3	36.4	37.7	39.0
1.50	33.8	35.1	36.0	37.0	38.1	39.2	40.4
1.75	42.9	43.5	44.0	44.6	45.3	46.1	47.0
2.00	50.0	50.2	50.5	50.8	51.3	51.9	52.5
2.50	60.0	60.0	60.1	60.2	60.4	60.7	61.0

Part III
Cost of Capital

Case 8
Mobile Energy, Inc.

In reviewing the latest financial results of Mobile Energy, Inc., (MEI), John Hamilton, vice–president for planning of MEI Industries, a subsidiary of MEI engaged in transportation services and real estate development, realized just how important these nonregulated activities had become to the parent of Mobile Electric Power, the utility serving the Mobile, Alabama, area. Although still accounting for less than 10 percent of the overall company's revenues, MEI Industries produced almost one–fifth of the holding company's operating income in 1990. While justifiably proud of the contribution his fast–growing operation made to the company in the last couple of years, he knew two recent investments were the primary cause of this profitability. He was also aware that the volatile nature of the transit business would make the return on future investments much less assured than these latest acquisitions which came with reliable, term contracts. Given the largely operational basis for his company's investment decisions in the past, Hamilton began to wonder whether the return expected on other current and future investments properly compensated the firm for the risk it would be assuming. As he continued to think about the implications, a number of questions popped into his head. He decided to give Kathryn Schultz, the treasurer of MEI, a call and discuss some of these points over lunch the next day.

What Hamilton learned was that there was a formal, though unwritten, procedure for estimating a risk–adjusted discount rate for use in the analysis of capital additions, and that this expected return, or "hurdle" rate, for investments was based on the overall holding company's cost of capital. The debt, and especially equity, components of this cost reflect risks associated with the operations and financing of the firm. However, a single rate was used for all potential projects—whether regulated or not, or whether having an apparent high– or low–degree of risk. While admitting that the risks associated with investments by MEI Industries were indeed very different, Schultz noted the historic dominance of the regulated utility, Mobile Electric Power, in the overall financial performance of MEI and that, until this year, the contribution of nonregulated activities was fairly insignificant. After some further discussion, she agreed with Hamilton that the whole issue merited a fresh look, and that she would set up a meeting next week with all interested parties to kickoff a review of their current estimating procedures.

Existing Procedure

As a starting point for the discussion of this issue, Robert May, a senior financial analyst and assistant to Kathryn Schultz, opened the meeting with a presentation of the company's current methodology. In large part, the discount rate used in the analysis of capital additions at MEI is based on the utility's "allowed" rate of return on equity. The most recent determination of this rate was in January of 1990, when the Alabama Public Service Commission granted Mobile Electric Power a rate increase designed to produce a 13.5 percent return on equity. This allowed rate of return on equity is combined then with the after–tax cost of new "AA"–rated utility bonds (the company's current rating) and new "AA"–rated preferred issues,

---

Sources: Data and information based on various publications, including S&P Stock Reports.

and weighted by its current capital structure (see EXHIBIT 1). The company reasoned that the rate of return on equity reflected the average risk of regulated business activities of the firm, which until recently accounted for over 90 percent of its income. An example of a recent calculation of this cost of capital, and thus the required return on potential new investments, is:

Source	Amount		Rate		Cost
Long–Term Debt	$675	×	9.6%(1–.34)	=	$43
Preferred Stock	555	×	9.1%	=	51
Common Equity	877	×	13.5%	=	118
Total Capital	$2,107				$212
Cost of Capital	$212/$2,107 = 10.1%				

At this point Hamilton raised a major concern regarding the use of an accounting rate of return, especially an "allowed" rate. In response, Schultz argued that investor (cash) returns were too unstable because of the inherent volatility of the stock market. She also pointed out that this 13.5 percent rate was consistent with the Commission's "allowed" returns of 13–14 percent for the company during the mid– to late–1980s. Also, unlike many regulated utilities where the lags in the implementation of regulated rates alone result in actual returns 1–2 percent below those allowed, MEI historically has achieved returns approximating those allowed because of especially effective management of rate requests. While this was probably true, Hamilton attributed the company's success more to the strong growth in industrial demand in its service area as well as the rapid expansion in nonregulated businesses in recent years. Anticipating this issue, May had prepared exhibits for this meeting showing the holding company's (accounting) return on equity, which averaged about 15 percent (see EXHIBIT 2), annually compounded, from 1985 to 1989, and one illustrating what investors had realized (market rate of return) during this period, which was over 20 percent (see EXHIBIT 3). He also interjected a reminder that the stock market in the 1980s, especially the latter part of the decade, was unusually bullish—in fact you'd have to go back to the 1950s or 1920s to see a similar run–up in stock prices.

Another question Hamilton had had that seemed appropriate to bring up at this time was with regard to the use of book values for the capital structure weights. He wondered why market values were not the appropriate basis, and further why an embedded structure was being used instead of the mix of funds that would be raised incrementally. It dawned on him then that, at market values, the embedded mix was even more conservative than indicated by the book value proportions. The obvious next question was what debt/equity mix did the company plan to use for new capital. As he began to wonder this out loud, he decided to let Schultz answer the previous question first since he was starting to get out of his "comfort zone" in his knowledge of corporate finance. Her answer to the capital structure weights question was essentially the same as it was to the rate of return question, that is, that market values fluctuate too much to be a reliable basis for an estimate of the cost of capital, and that the embedded capital structure and accounting rates of return were consistent measures. May added the issue of capital structure to that of book vs. market rate of return on his list of topics to investigate.

The discussion then turned to the possibility of more than one discount rate for use in an increasingly wide range of investment projects. In particular, Hamilton noted the obvious distinction between regulated and nonregulated activities, and that the risk, if significantly different, necessitated more than one "hurdle" rate. Again, while admitting that there were clearly some risk differences between the two operations, Schultz countered that the overall cost of capital represented an average of these risks, and further questioned how a reliable measure could be estimated that would properly gauge project risk. While not having the answer, Hamilton began to describe how different the risk was in their recent foray into the production of natural gas, or ocean–going transit, vs. selling electricity to an established base of geographically stationary utility customers. Both parties looked at May, who was already busy scribbling on his legal pad.

In order to understand more about the nature of risk throughout the firm, a little background on the company and its operations may be of help.

Background

With the change in state law in 1985 permitting utilities to engage in nonregulated businesses, Mobile Electric Power formed the holding company Mobile Energy, Inc., and launched the subsidiary MEI Industries to coordinate and develop the supply and delivery of coal used in the company's generation of electricity. Early in this period, the company purchased two Tennessee coal mines, a towing company providing river barging services, and a transloading facility in the modern port of Mobile. More recently, the subsidiary has expanded into ocean–going transit, the production of natural gas, and various industrial real estate ventures.

With the completion of the Tennessee–Tombigbee Waterway, which allows barge traffic from Mobile to the Great Lakes and Pittsburgh, port–related activities offer significant growth potential for these nonregulated businesses. Additionally, the regulated electric utility serves the highly industrialized Mobile metropolitan area, consisting of approximately 3,000 square miles and some 22 municipalities in Mobile and Baldwin Counties. More than 400 manufacturing industries are represented in its service area, including paper and paper products, shipbuilding, chemicals, lumber products, computer hardware and software, textiles, and seafood processing. Shipping out of Alabama's major seaport is also a major industry, and more recently, oil and gas production have become major growth industries in the southern part of the state. The upshot is that both the regulated and nonregulated businesses of MEI show considerable promise, and with a continued positive regulatory environment, they will offer many potentially profitable investment opportunities in the future.

Other Cost of Capital Issues

With this sense of the business risks of MEI, and the major issues that Schultz and Hamilton had raised in their discussion, Robert May knew that the responsibility would fall on him to provide sound financial arguments for whatever approach was developed, and to quantify the estimating procedure to the satisfaction of not only Schultz and Hamilton, but ultimately to Douglas Breidel, the senior vice–president of finance for MEI. As he sat there with the meeting winding down, he wanted to be sure that he understood exactly what was expected of him, and whether there was any other information that he needed or issues that should be discussed while Schultz and Hamilton were in the same room.

From the discussion of risk, and his formal training in finance, he immediately thought of "beta." He was well aware of all the theoretical and practical problems with estimating and using betas, but with a quick "back of the envelope" calculation with MEI's company beta of .70, the risk–free rate at just under 6 percent, and average market returns in the recent past of high "teens" to high "twenties," he came up with an estimated cost of equity in the 15–20 percent range. This showed some promise, but he wasn't quite sure yet how he would apply this concept to different businesses and projects throughout the holding company—and how he would be able to demonstrate that the overall cost of capital indeed reflected an average of various company and project risks. One estimate he would need, if he pursued this possibility, was the dollar proportions of new capital projects between the regulated and nonregulated businesses of MEI. After a few moment's reflection, Schultz suggested an 85%/15% split.

From this thought, he logically shifted to the issue of the degree of leverage. In addition to the discussion that had taken place on book vs. market values, and future mix vs. historic proportions, he started thinking about whether different debt/equity proportions should be assumed for the regulated and nonregulated businesses. They did have very different business risks. When he brought this point up, both Schultz and Hamilton agreed that MEI Industries did have alternative sources of debt (and to some extent, through joint ventures, equity as well).

Finally, Schultz asked if there was anything else he needed. May said no, but what he was really thinking was, "Yes, everything else I haven't thought of yet." With this, the meeting broke up and May was expected to provide a recommendation in approximately two to three weeks.

Discussion Questions

1. If the company decides to stay with the current, single–rate approach, what suggestions would you make to improve the methodology?

2. What effects would the continued use of a single, average cost of capital–based rate have on the company over time?

3. Discuss some of the advantages and disadvantages, both theoretical and practical, of adopting multiple hurdle rates. Should these rates apply to divisions, or to specific projects, or both?

4. What are some of the approaches you could try to measure capital component costs, especially the cost of equity? How can these be applied with multiple hurdle rates? How should the various component costs be weighted?

5. There are betas and there are betas. Explain the various applications of the beta concept. What are some of the theoretical and practical limitations in the use of betas?

6. Explain what would be your recommendation to the company regarding the use of multiple hurdle rates, and how, specifically, would it be implemented and administered?

7. What additional information would be useful for this analysis?

Exhibit 1
Mobile Electric, Inc.
Statement of Financial Condition, 1985–1989

($ millions)	1985	1986	1987	1988	1989
Assets					
Cash	21	45	78	86	135
Other Current Assets	220	223	241	248	252
Total Current Assets	241	268	319	334	387
Fixed Assets & Other	1,798	1,845	1,951	1,981	2,000
TOTAL ASSETS	2,039	2,113	2,270	2,315	2,387
Liabilities and Equity					
Total Current Liabilities	133	136	235	211	236
Other Long–Term Liabilities	23	24	24	40	44
Long–Term Debt	644	685	660	684	675
Preferred Stock	514	513	559	552	555
Common Equity	725	755	792	828	877
Total Invested Capital	1,883	1,953	2,011	2,064	2,107
TOTAL LIABILITIES AND EQUITY	2,039	2,113	2,270	2,315	2,387

Exhibit 2
Mobile Electric, Inc.
Statement of Operations, 1985–1989

($ millions)	1985	1986	1987	1988	1989
Operating Revenues	886	902	970	1,034	1,060
– Operating Expenses	563	575	618	694	694
Operating Income	323	327	352	340	366
– Depreciation	82	93	101	106	112
+ Other Income	10	8	5	15	14
EBIT	251	242	256	249	268
– Interest Expense	59	55	61	63	59
Earnings Before Taxes	192	187	195	186	209
– Income Taxes	87	83	78	60	71
NET INCOME	105	104	117	126	138
Return on Equity	14.5%	13.8%	14.8%	15.9%	15.7%

(1985–1989 Compound Annual Rate – 14.9%)

Exhibit 3
Mobile Electric, Inc.
Per Share Market Data, 1980–1989

Year	Book Value	Average Price	P/E Ratio	EPS	DPS	Return on Equity
1989	$15.45	$25.750	11	$2.36	$1.495	18.5%
1988	14.59	23.000	11	2.13	1.400	1.7%
1987	13.98	24.000	12	1.95	1.320	13.8%
1986	13.34	22.250	13	1.73	1.240	45.7%
1985	12.86	16.125	9	1.79	1.160	26.9%
1984	12.13	13.625	7	1.86	1.080	23.8%
1983	11.26	11.875	8	1.57	1.000	30.4%
1982	10.68	9.875	8	1.25	0.920	10.7%
1981	10.46	9.750	7	1.50	0.840	34.5%
1980	9.83	7.875	5	1.56	0.765	–

(1985–1989 Compound Annual Rate – 20.5%)

Case 9
Northern Woods Campers, Inc.

The prospect of a new cabinetry facility was an exciting development for the company. Northern Woods Campers, Inc., manufactures travel trailers of various lengths and configurations in Berrien Springs, Michigan, and also fabricates camper/travel vans. The wood trim and cabinetry in these units adds style and functionality valued by its customers, but at a significant cost. With the market becoming so price competitive in the last few years, the ability to control costs with the addition of a new, efficient production facility may be a necessity, rather than just a "nice–to have." That was the thinking of James Thompson, Northern Woods' president. But the lack of an analysis of return on investment in the proposal he was reviewing gave him some pause. As he was thinking about this point, it occurred to him that he didn't even know what would be an acceptable return, as a minimum. What was the company's cost of capital? He wrote these questions across the top of the report and sent it to Charles Robbins, his vice–president of finance. A million dollar addition may not seem like a major expansion, but to a company with less than $3 million total in fixed assets, the potential profitability of this investment needed documentation.

Company and Industry

Northern Woods operates in a highly cyclical industry and is vulnerable to the level of interest rates and gasoline prices in particular. While these factors have been well behaved in recent years, the economy remained weak for the second year in a row. Finally, 1993 should bring a rebound in camper sales that should continue for the next few years (see EXHIBIT 1 for operating results in the last few years). It is during this sales period that the company hopes to profit from the proposed cabinetry facility.

The idea for this project came from the company's success with its sofa/chair venture a few years ago. When a major supplier of its seating equipment was flirting with bankruptcy awhile back, Northern Woods provided the infusion of cash, and eventually acquired the firm. The experience was a good one all around, giving the company a reliable supply of quality products at substantial savings, and it saved the jobs of a couple hundred dedicated workers in the Bowling Green, Ohio, facility.

This investment would involve an addition to its main plant and its internal capabilities in woodworking. It also would allow for some rearrangement of its plant layout and the attendant benefits of improvements to its entire production–inventory system. The company's historic utilization of fixed assets, compared to the industry, is shown in EXHIBIT 2.

Sources: Data and information based on various publications, including S&P Stock Reports, RMA Annual Statement Studies, S&P Analysts' Handbook, Value Line, Dow–Jones Irwin.

Financial Structure and Costs

But the risks in this volatile industry are ever present, witnessed by the complete aversion to long–term debt by Northern Woods' competitors. And even with its debt at less than 10 percent of total invested capital (see EXHIBIT 3), the best rate the company can get is the equivalent of the "BBB" rate. The historic behavior of this rate is provided in EXHIBIT 4, together with some stock market information.

The nature of this industry makes the reliance on equity for most of a company's capital needs almost unavoidable, and for Northern Woods, this has been all internally generated equity. Add to this that its stock, while public, is closely held and not actively traded. Comparisons with the stock behavior of publicly traded competitors (see EXHIBIT 5) is hampered by varying struggles of their own with this recession. The use of market data, then, to estimate its cost of equity, is somewhat problematic.

This was the dilemma facing Charles Robbins in his effort to answer his boss's question. He himself wondered how well the company's stock related to the market, and to the camper/travel van industry in particular. The quality of his cost of capital estimate and perhaps even the decision on the plant addition would hinge on the answer to this question.

Discussion Questions

1. From the data provided, does it seem that Northern Woods' "market" price is a true measure of its market value?

2. How has this company performed in terms of its book return on equity, compared to the industry? Calculate a value–weighted industry price indicator series (index) including Northern Woods. How well has Northern Woods' share price tracked the industry? What is the relationship of the industry to the market (S&P 500)?

3. Would a price–weighted or unweighted (equal weighted) index for the industry be superior to a value–weighted index? How does Northern Woods compare on these bases (with the Dow–Jones Industrial Average and the Value Line Composite Index, respectively).

4. Calculate a market, equity beta for each of these publicly traded travel trailer/motor home companies using annual data over the ten–year period. How do these compare to their published estimates, which are based on frequent observations over the most recent five years (Coachmen, 0.87; Fleetwood, 1.28; Rexhall, n/a; Thor, 0.95; Winnebago, 1.27)? Northern Woods, calculated on the same basis as the published estimates, would be 0.73. Are betas useful in determining the cost of equity in this industry?

5. Estimate the company's cost of equity capital.

6. What is the proper debt/equity mix for a cost of capital calculation? What is Northern Woods' cost of capital?

7. What additional information would be useful for this analysis?

Exhibit 1
Statements of Operations
1988–1992

($mm) Year Ended October 31	1988	1989	1990	1991	1992
Revenues	73.8	69.4	67.4	57.4	55.5
– Operating Expenses	71.6	67.7	66.2	56.9	54.8
Operating Income	2.2	1.7	1.2	0.5	0.7
– Depreciation	0.3	0.4	0.3	0.3	0.3
EBIT	1.9	1.3	0.9	0.2	0.4
– Interest Expense	0.1	0.1	0.1	0.1	0.1
Earnings Before Taxes	1.8	1.2	0.8	0.1	0.3
+ Other Income	0.2	0.4	0.4	0.1	2.1
Net Before Taxes	2.0	1.6	1.2	0.2	2.4
– Income Taxes	0.7	0.6	0.4	0.1	0.9
NET INCOME	1.3	1.0	0.8	0.1	1.5
CAPITAL EXPENDITURES	0.4	0.4	0.3	0.1	0.4

Exhibit 2
Fixed Asset Utilization
1988–1992

	1988	1989	1990	1991	1992
Fixed Assets/Total Assets					
Northern Woods	19.2	15.1	15.3	13.8	13.8
Industry	20.4	28.9	25.3	26.3	23.2
Sales/Fixed Assets					
Northern Woods	21.1	24.8	24.1	22.1	21.3
Industry	22.8	15.8	18.9	15.7	16.9

Exhibit 3
Statements of Financial Condition
1988–1992

($mm) Year Ended October 31	1988	1989	1990	1991	1992
Assets					
Cash	4.6	6.1	6.1	6.5	9.3
Other Current Assets	10.1	9.6	9.4	9.7	6.9
Total Current Assets	14.7	15.7	15.5	16.2	16.2
Long–Term Assets	3.5	2.8	2.8	2.6	2.6
TOTAL ASSETS	18.2	18.5	18.3	18.8	18.8
Liabilities and Equity					
Total Current Liabilities	6.6	5.8	4.7	5.2	3.6
Long–Term Debt	1.0	1.1	1.2	1.2	1.3
Common Equity	10.6	11.6	12.4	12.4	13.9
Total Invested Capital	11.6	12.7	13.6	13.6	15.2
TOTAL LIABILITIES AND EQUITY	18.2	18.5	18.3	18.8	18.8

Exhibit 4
Financial Market Indicators
1983–1992

Year	"BBB" Rate	Dow–Jones Industrials	Value Line Composite	S&P 500		
				Price Index	Earnings	Dividends
1983	12.7%	1190.34	181.88	160.41	14.03	7.09
1984	14.0	1178.48	165.56	160.46	16.64	7.53
1985	12.2	1328.23	199.87	186.84	14.61	7.90
1986	10.5	1792.76	210.06	236.34	14.48	8.28
1987	10.8	2275.99	187.60	286.83	17.50	8.81
1988	10.8	2060.82	228.45	265.79	23.75	9.73
1989	10.5	2508.91	267.46	322.84	22.87	11.05
1990	10.8	2678.94	224.75	334.59	21.34	12.10
1991	10.5	2929.33	217.22	376.18	15.97	12.20
1992	9.2	3284.29	251.54	415.74	19.09	12.38
1993e	8.75	–	–	–	–	–

Exhibit 5
Earnings, Dividends, Book Value Per Share,
Market Price, Number of Shares
1983–1992

	83	84	85	86	87	88	89	90	91	92
Northern Woods										
Earnings/Share	−0.51	0.20	0.40	0.82	1.25	0.85	0.70	0.54	0.07	0.99
Dividends/Share	0.00	0.00	0.00	0.00	0.00	0.00	0.00	0.00	0.00	0.00
Book Value/Share	3.86	3.80	4.20	5.13	6.81	6.93	8.12	8.37	8.37	9.17
Average Price	7.19	4.56	5.06	8.56	8.56	7.69	6.63	5.50	5.81	6.88
# of Shares	1.37	1.50	1.50	1.46	1.44	1.53	1.43	1.48	1.48	1.52
Coachmen Inds										
Earnings/Share	2.71	1.70	0.45	0.53	−0.22	0.52	−0.31	−1.55	−1.88	1.13
Dividends/Share	0.25	0.40	0.40	0.40	0.40	0.40	0.40	0.27	0.08	0.08
Book Value/Share	9.37	10.41	10.17	9.94	9.12	10.07	9.37	7.33	5.68	6.78
Average Price	25.56	21.00	15.56	15.19	10.81	10.13	8.69	5.94	5.75	11.56
# of Shares	8.45	8.65	8.44	8.30	8.18	7.50	7.42	7.42	7.13	7.17
Fleetwood Inds										
Earnings/Share	0.53	1.15	1.14	0.94	1.04	1.53	2.21	1.62	0.88	1.23
Dividends/Share	0.15	0.18	0.22	0.26	0.30	0.32	0.38	0.42	0.44	0.47
Book Value/Share	2.87	3.92	5.51	6.89	8.28	10.92	12.57	12.49	12.39	14.32
Average Price	14.94	11.25	11.56	13.56	11.50	10.94	13.19	11.25	14.31	18.69
# of Shares	56.04	55.57	47.02	41.81	38.17	31.50	31.90	33.95	34.55	32.68
Rexhall Inds										
Earnings/Share	n/a	n/a	n/a	n/a	0.12	0.49	1.12	0.29	−0.48	−0.61
Dividends/Share	n/a	n/a	n/a	n/a	0.00	0.00	0.00	0.00	0.00	0.00
Book Value/Share	n/a	n/a	n/a	n/a	0.16	0.64	4.34	3.77	3.30	2.72
Average Price	n/a	n/a	n/a	n/a	n/a	n/a	8.06	6.88	5.44	3.00
# of Shares	n/a	n/a	n/a	n/a	1.92	1.88	1.94	2.41	2.40	2.39
Thor Industries										
Earnings/Share	0.47	0.64	0.61	0.77	0.97	0.75	0.43	0.47	0.08	1.15
Dividends/Share	0.00	0.00	0.00	0.00	0.00	0.08	0.08	0.08	0.08	0.09
Book Value/Share	0.83	1.93	2.44	3.19	4.26	4.89	5.34	5.69	5.83	9.73
Average Price	n/a	4.31	5.38	9.25	11.38	8.25	7.88	5.81	10.75	20.06
# of Shares	6.85	7.19	7.59	7.61	7.59	7.67	7.58	7.19	7.00	7.30
Winnebago Inds										
Earnings/Share	0.63	1.10	0.71	0.77	0.78	0.11	−0.19	−0.72	−0.65	−0.07
Dividends/Share	0.10	0.10	0.20	0.20	0.30	0.40	0.40	0.10	0.00	0.00
Book Value/Share	3.85	4.87	5.33	5.94	6.12	5.91	5.30	4.49	3.31	2.80
Average Price	17.19	11.63	14.69	14.88	11.44	9.56	6.94	3.94	4.50	6.56
# of Shares	24.92	25.27	25.49	25.58	25.64	24.55	24.74	24.72	25.08	25.71

Part IV
Financial Policy

Case 10
O'Malley Steel, Inc.

The U.S. steel industry has undergone tumultuous changes over the last two decades—from virtual extinction, to a modest (though thriving) competitor, to a recessionary victim, to once again a functioning domestic industry. Although the industry, and its strongest participants, are hardly out of the woods at this point, they can now be described as economically viable and worthy niche competitors.

Against this backdrop, the Johnson and O'Malley Steel Company was formed in the late seventies as a joint venture of two struggling regional integrated steel producers. Besides the obvious advantage of a substantial new investment in plant and equipment, the primary consideration was to reduce the number of employees, and thereby the cost of producing raw steel, by changing work rules and the relationship between management and labor. Although still union organized, workers were more directly involved in production and operations decisions, including even appropriate investments in fixed assets. This cooperative arrangement was really quite radical for its time and especially in the steel industry. In addition to opening a new era of management–labor relations, it also helped launch the minimill trend in the steel industry. The Johnson and O'Malley Steel Company invested in, and transformed, a dying facility in the heart of Pennsylvania steel country, into a quasi–minimill, and the company has been consistently profitable since the mid–1980s. The firm became a publicly traded company in July 1988, and with a recent stock issue, is now listed on the NYSE as O'Malley Steel, Inc. (OMS).

Steel Production

In order to understand the company's products and markets, it is necessary to begin with the nature of the steel industry. While seemingly quite straightforward, the production of steel and the nature of the industry are really quite complex and diverse. The terminology alone, from billets and blooms to annealing and cold rolling, has sent many a banker and financial analyst to language school just to interpret the industry's operational performance, much less to evaluate it. Although the following is only a broad overview, some background is necessary to understand the firm's activities.

First, there are five major types of steel: carbon steels, alloy steels, stainless steels, tool steels, and HSLA (high–strength, low–alloy) steels. Carbon steels contain very small amounts of alloying elements, manganese, silicon, and copper, and have a carbon content of 0.08 percent to 1.7 percent. They make up 85 percent of total raw steel production. Low–carbon steels are used primarily for flat–rolled products, which can be formed and welded, for machines, auto bodies, ship hulls, and most structural steel for buildings. Alloy steels contain specific percentages of vanadium, molybdenum, and other elements as well as larger amounts of manganese, silicon, and copper than carbon grades contain. Their greater strength, corrosion–resistance, and special electrical attributes make them suitable for tools and equipment in the auto, construction, and various industrial and electrical equipment industries. These make up approximately

Sources: Data and information based on various publications including S&P Stock Reports, S&P Industry Surveys.

13 percent of industry output. Stainless steels account for less than 2 percent, and are well known for possessing the properties of high rust resistance, unusual strength, and resistance to temperature changes. Aerospace, petrochemical, and medical equipment industries are the primary users of stainless steel. Tool steels are alloyed with tungsten and molybdenum for extreme strength and hardiness, and find applications in metalworking industries, especially cutting and shaping parts of power–driven machines. HSLA steels represent a family of hybrids, where both strength and weight are crucial, such as in automobiles, railroad freight cars, and commercial buildings.

Second, the nature of steel production involves iron ore and scrap, and through the molting in a basic–oxygen or electric furnace, produces semi–finished (slabs, billets, and blooms) or finished (rods and bars, pipe, plates, strips, and sheets) products. The minimill operation, in contrast to integrated steel producers, differs essentially by dispensing with the iron–making steps and begins with steel scrap, flux, and occasionally directly reduced iron.

Finally, in order to forecast the potential demand for steel products, long–term outlooks must be made for plant and equipment additions for all industries (the real estate industry and construction equipment in particular), machine tools, agricultural equipment, electrical, specialty manufactures, etc. Trends in technology and substitute materials (plastic, aluminum, ceramics) must also be factored in, as should new federal government initiatives, including environmental legislation.

O'Malley Steel Products and Markets

The company owns and operates a technologically advanced steel mill which produces bar and medium–sized structural steel products from scrap steel. It is the prototypical "minimill."

The O'Malley facility operates two electric arc furnaces and continuously casts billets for the plant's bar mill and medium section mill. Products include structural beams, special quality rounds, reinforcing bars, structural and merchant angles, channels, and flats. Bar mill products account for 40 percent of sales, on a tonnage basis, and 60 percent from structural mill products. Their principal market is the construction industry, but they also sell to railroads, defense and automobile industries, mobile home manufacturers, and the energy industry.

The company has enjoyed healthy growth for most of the 1980s (see EXHIBIT 1 for the most recent five years) and played its part in driving Inland Steel and USX–U.S. Steel from many of its markets. This has positioned the company to capture market share and take advantage of economies of scale with the large section mill. The proposed investment would allow the company to enter the market for larger structural products, with a 500,000 ton–per–year capacity. In total, this would give O'Malley Steel the capability of rolling 2,000,000 tons per year.

Investment Financing

Recent changes in the competitive landscape have made this investment decision an easy one. The problem here is only with how it should be financed. Specifically, the company is considering debt, another equity issue, or perhaps some combination of the two. In discussing these possibilities with its investment bank, the probable terms of each type of issue were provided (see EXHIBIT 2).

The actual size of the plant addition is $125 million, plus needed additions to net working capital over the next three years (see EXHIBIT 3). The necessary financing should be net of internally generated funds, which can be estimated from the current sales forecast of $485 million in 1991, and a more modest 7 percent per year thereafter. These estimates reflect some gains in markets and market share, but are diminished by the current outlook for the steel industry, due to sluggishness of the economy, foreign competition, and fierce competition from plastics, aluminum, glass, and ceramics industries.

Making the Call

The privilege of making this decision rests with Mike Moran, the CEO and operating officer. He began his career like many young GIs after World War II working long hours, in blistering heat, for subsistence wages, in the plants and mills in the industrial heartland, and truly felt fortunate to be working. With hard work and a little luck he was able to rise through the ranks over a 40–year career to his present position. Through it all, he has never forgotten what it takes to make steel, and even today makes regular visits to the young Mike Morans in his mill. Thus, while he certainly knows the business, literally from the bottom up, he knows as much about finance as his investment banker knows about pig iron and fluxes.

Fortunately for him, both his president, Arlen Pierce, and his chief financial officer, Julie Erlenbach, have financial backgrounds and have served the company well in a most challenging environment. He has complete confidence in their abilities and judgments but he has been presented with a dilemma. From preliminary discussions with the investment banking firm the company has retained, another stock issue was recommended (see EXHIBIT 4 for recent market data), while his own people have advised a debt offering. The stock issue was advised in order to reduce the company's leverage and produce a higher earnings per share and, therefore, shareholder value. However, Mr. Pierce and Ms. Erlenbach felt quite strongly that the debt issue would produce a higher earnings per share and that the advantages of debt outweighed its disadvantages, and the advantages of an equity issue. Since Mr. Moran is clearly handicapped in this area, he has decided to request a detailed listing and argument of the advantages and disadvantages of each alternative.

Discussion Questions

1. Prepare a three–year financial projection assuming the company invests in the large section mill. What are the financing requirements?

2. Since there is some debate over which financing option would result in the highest earnings per share, prepare an analysis showing this. On what basis could each side arrive at the conclusion they have?

3. What would be the financial condition of the firm over the projection period under each option?

4. Detail the advantages and disadvantages of each option.

5. Consider the degrees of operating and financial leverage. How does this influence the decision?

6. What additional information would be useful for this analysis?

Exhibit 1
O'Malley Steel, Inc.
Statement of Operations, 1986–1990

($mm)	1986	1987	1988	1989	1990e
Operating Revenues	297	319	376	451	404
– Cost of Goods Sold	214	220	252	298	291
Gross Margin	83	99	124	153	113
– Operating Expenses	26	39	44	50	49
Operating Income	57	60	80	103	64
– Depreciation	22	24	22	18	20
+ Other Income	2	7	3	5	6
EBIT	37	43	61	90	50
– Interest Expense	22	19	17	15	13
Earnings Before Taxes	15	24	44	75	37
– Income Taxes	6	11	13	26	13
NET INCOME	9	13	31	49	24

Exhibit 2
Debt and Equity Issue Terms

Debt Financing	Equity Financing
20–year bonds	Common stock
"B" rating	"B–" rating
$1,000 denomination	Par Value – $1
11.5% coupon	$0.20/share dividend
Estimated price – 102.5	Estimated price – $11.25
Sinking fund in year 6 (.067)	Full voting rights
Issuance costs:	Issuance costs:
Fixed – $2.5 million	Fixed – $2.5 million
Variable – 2%	Variable – 5%

Exhibit 3
O'Malley Steel, Inc.
Statement of Financial Condition, 1986–1990

($ mm)	1986	1987	1988	1989	1990e
Assets					
Cash	1	15	16	46	32
Other Current Assets	96	102	103	113	119
Total Current Assets	97	117	119	159	151
Fixed Assets & Other	213	204	204	215	232
TOTAL ASSETS	310	321	323	374	383
Liabilities and Equity					
Total Current Liabilities	55	59	56	69	63
Other Long–Term Liabilities	15	28	38	47	45
Long–Term Debt	158	140	120	95	94
Preferred Stock	12	11	0	0	0
Common Equity	70	83	109	163	181
Total Invested Capital	240	234	229	258	275
TOTAL LIABILITIES AND EQUITY	310	321	323	374	383

Exhibit 4
O'Malley Steel, Inc.
Per Share Market Data, 1987–1990

Year	Book Value	EPS	DPS	Average Price	P/E Ratio
1991e	–	–	0.20*	–	–
1990e	5.58	0.74	0.125	11.875	16.0
1989	5.21	1.57	0.100	12.875	8.2
1988	3.48	0.98	NIL	NA	NA
1987	NA	NIL	NIL	NA	NA

* Recent policy decision.

Case 11
Boyesen Industries, Inc.

Stockholders' meetings are usually rather perfunctory affairs. Each management speaker presents his or her assessment of some facet of the previous year's business, in turn, and as a part of a well–orchestrated overall company story line. The planted questions pop up, on cue, and serve to punctuate the intended direction and tone of the remarks. Occasionally, something unexpected will come up but the tight control of the rules of order, and the podium, quickly return the proceedings to the carefully scripted and rehearsed presentation by management. And finally, they end on a positive and reassuring note about the diligence with which stockholders interests will be protected by management against a future of uncertainties. At least that is the way they are suppose to go.

Robert Conroy, a freshly minted MBA, and a recent hire by Boyesen Industries, was looking forward to his first stockholders' meeting, and the performance of his boss, senior vice–president of finance, Gordon Summerfield. In his short tenure with the company, Mr. Conroy had been given the opportunity to sit in on all the planning sessions as well as some of the rehearsals. He was asked from time to time how effectively various points were being made and once, even what his opinion was on a matter that was being discussed. Thus he felt a somewhat vested interest in this meeting, despite an obviously peripheral role.

The Company

Boyesen Industries is a manufacturer of textile mill products and apparel, primarily moderately priced, private label underwear and leisure outerwear. A former textile mill, the company has succeeded over the last 15 years in integrating vertically to the point now where approximately 90 percent of its revenues are derived from completed apparel. This transformation has been quite orderly, as evidenced by its 3–, 5–, and 10–year sales growth rates of 14.9 percent, 12.9 percent, and 11.5 percent, respectively. Being in both the textile and apparel industries, surprisingly, it has no real horror stories to tell. Rather, it has been consistently profitable, has achieved healthy growth in brutally competitive industries, and enjoys flattering stock valuations by security analysts and investors alike. EXHIBITS 1 and 2 provide evidence of this from its financial statements, with confirmation from market data, provided in EXHIBIT 3.

All of this would suggest that whatever the company was doing, it should keep doing it. This was not going to be the usual schmooze with the shareholders, however; the company had apparently committed the cardinal sin of being out of touch with its stockholders. This was a particularly grievous fault in that only 6 percent of the 40 million plus shares outstanding were held by individuals, the remaining being almost evenly divided between the founder's family and a group of large institutional investors.

Sources: Data and information based on various publications, including S&P Stock Reports, S&P Industry Surveys.

Year–End Stockholders' Meeting

Uncharacteristically, 1991 was an off–year for Boyesen in a number of ways. In order to rebound from sluggish sales in 1990, the company discounted some of its lines and spent heavily on marketing in 1991, causing double–digit declines in earnings. Other factors contributed to this temporary setback, but every indicator suggested a return to growth, in fact at an even higher expected growth rate of 14–15 percent.

Richard Lee, Boyesen's charming, avuncular chairman and CEO, was relating these circumstances to his audience and producing the sympathy and understanding he wanted, in order to set the stage for Mr. Summerfield's presentation of the financial results. But as Mr. Summerfield was concluding, the issue of dividend payout came up a second time. A group of the family shareholders persisted in their questioning of why dividend payments could not be higher. A large institutional investor fanned the flames with her observation that over the last several years, actual growth was below sustainable growth, indicating an investment problem. Although civil, the debate continued on for another 20 minutes, but without resolution. Mr. Lee finally jumped in, promising a careful study of the issue, and directed the proceedings to the next scheduled speaker.

Between the conclusion of the formal meeting and the dinner that evening, Richard Lee reviewed his company's performance and some industry data he had requested from Robert Conroy (see EXHIBIT 4). The need, or justification, for a higher payout was still not apparent to him. But he willingly discussed the issue at dinner in spite of his personal reservations. Repeatedly through the evening, he reassured his investors that the company would study the issue thoroughly and do whatever would maximize the price of the stock. At 1:30 p.m., the day mercifully ended, and he collapsed in his bed. As he dropped off, he was thinking that he had had one or two better days.

Dividend Model

Two weeks later, Richard Lee, Gordon Summerfield, and Robert Conroy met to discuss the dividend payment issue. What Mr. Lee wanted specifically was a model which would allow him to "see" the relationships among the relevant variables, and then to use it to determine what dividend policy made the most sense, and specifically, one that was sustainable. That task fell to young Conroy, with the guidance of Gordon Summerfield, who was doctorally qualified in the field.

Mr. Lee asked what an appropriate time frame was, and it was decided that a couple of months would be needed. With that, Robert Conroy accepted an assignment that he knew could materially affect his career at Boyesen Industries.

Discussion Questions

1. Is there a theory of dividends? What are common practices of U.S. firms regarding dividend payments?

2. How would you summarize dividend policy in the textile manufacturing industry?

3. Is anything wrong with Boyesen's current dividend payment pattern?

4. Looking at the last three to five years of change, what is the apparent target capital structure? Given a target debt/equity mix, equity turnover, and book return on equity at historical rates, what dividend growth rate can be sustained? Detail this projection further with expected book values per share, P/E ratios, and dividend yields, given total market returns for the company's stockholders at the same rate as they have averaged over the last five years. Explain the interrelationships among these variables.

5. Among the various factors which, if altered, could bolster the dividend payout, which ones are feasible?

6. What dividend policy would maximize the value of the stock, and how would you explain this to the company's shareholders?

7. What additional information would be useful for this analysis?

Exhibit 1
Statements of Operations
1986–1991

($mm) Year Ended December 31	1986	1987	1988	1989	1990	1991
Revenues	438	480	531	688	714	805
– Operating Expenses	331	369	402	523	537	640
Operating Income	107	111	129	165	177	165
– Depreciation	23	26	33	45	51	57
EBIT	84	85	96	120	126	108
– Interest Expense	4	7	9	16	19	18
Earnings Before Taxes	80	78	87	104	107	90
+ Other Income	0	2	(1)	(1)	3	1
Net Before Taxes	80	80	86	103	110	91
– Income Taxes	37	34	32	38	42	34
NET INCOME	43	46	54	65	68	57

Exhibit 2
Statements of Financial Condition
1986–1991

($mm) Year Ended December 31	1986	1987	1988	1989	1990	1991
Assets						
Cash	34	58	13	76	13	13
Other Current Assets	146	161	197	251	321	314
Total Current Assets	180	219	210	327	334	327
Long–Term Assets	171	226	351	394	461	491
TOTAL ASSETS	351	445	561	721	795	818
Liabilities and Equity						
Total Current Liabilities	32	56	86	60	85	72
Other Long–Term Liabilities	1	2	3	5	7	9
Long–Term Debt	38	74	84	205	191	180
Other Long–Term Capital	32	33	43	49	56	54
Common Equity	248	280	345	402	456	503
Total Invested Capital	318	387	472	656	703	737
TOTAL LIABILITIES AND EQUITY	351	445	561	721	795	818

Exhibit 3
Per Share and Market Data
1986–1991

	1986	1987	1988	1989	1990	1991
Earnings/Share	$1.08	1.17	1.36	1.57	1.65	1.38
Dividends/Share	$0.16	0.19	0.23	0.28	0.32	0.32
Price – High	$19.625	20.500	17.750	26.500	31.000	36.250
– Low	$9.250	10.625	11.375	15.625	16.000	19.750

Exhibit 4
Sample Industry Data

Average 5 Yr.	Fruit of the Loom	Garan	Kellwood	Oshkosh B'Gosh	Phillps Van Heus.	VF Corp.
Sales Growth	18.6%	6.8	9.9	13.0	11.9	13.8
Earnings Growth	208.1%	28.9	(2.0)	2.7	9.1	4.5
Payout Ratio	0.0%	45	47	24	17	41
Pretax RORevenue	5.9%	5.4	2.9	9.1	3.5	5.9
Pretax ROAssets	3.9%	8.1	5.3	18.2	7.4	8.2
Pretax ROEquity	25.8%	11.4	12.2	24.5	34.0	16.8
Debt/Capital	76.0%	13	39	25	55	37
Price/Earnings	10x	12x	13x	15x	10x	13x

Case 12
Johanek Corporation

Jack Johanek has always seen the silver lining in the frequently cloudy homebuilding industry in which his firm participates. Hurricane Andrew was just the most recent example of a setback that the company worked through and emerged stronger than ever. As a major builder of moderately priced single– and multi–family housing in the South, principally in Florida, Texas, and Arizona, the company incurred its share of lawsuits from the killer storm. But its proactive response in helping people rebuild their homes and their lives resulted in a 30 percent jump in revenues from its homebuilding business. It also helped expand significantly the financial services company it launched a few years ago, which includes a mortgage company, a title insurer, and a general property and casualty affiliate. Typically, it will build new housing, then arrange mortgage financing, title and home insurance, and even provide closing services for its buyers. Overall, revenues and income in Fiscal 1993 are at record levels (see EXHIBIT 1).

Other Company Interests

In recent years when homebuilding was down, Johanek Corporation aggressively developed its property management services of apartments and condominiums, but also with a number of existing shopping centers and small office buildings. Additionally, it constructed, invested in, and managed many neighborhood centers in the late 1980s until the glutted marketplace made that business no longer attractive. The company is also the exclusive builder of franchised motor inns for a successful regional motel chain. And as an outgrowth of its planned communities, it has ventured into, literally through joint ventures, golf and recreational facilities, and retirement developments.

Even with this continued growth and diversity in its building activities, the fastest growing segment of its revenues and earnings are mortgage banking and financial services. What is particularly intriguing about this to Jack Johanek is that there is a real scale factor to this business and he believes that the company is rapidly approaching the flash point of what he sees as potentially explosive growth. But to achieve this potential, the company needs to invest heavily in its computer processing capabilities over the next several years.

Computing Capability Alternatives

Dennis Stanton, Johanek's director of information systems, studied the issue of computing capability in great detail, and came to the conclusion that a system significantly larger than the one they currently have was needed to manage the expected volume of new business. From this work, he developed a list of specifications and capabilities for prospective vendors. Within 60 days, the company had six concrete proposals for a new computer system. Two were clearly out of line in terms of price/performance, and the

---

Sources: Data and information based on various publications, including S&P Stock Reports.

other four were invited to make presentations. All four pitches were highly polished, informative, and created some genuine excitement about the types of products and services the company would be able to provide with a new system. But the level of service was a serious concern with one of the companies and a second was eliminated after a routine check of client references. The finalists then were ACI Computer, Johanek's current provider of computer services, with their AC 1170, and Century Information Systems, the industry leader in financial services systems, with their Century 9010 model.

As these final alternatives became clear, Johanek's treasurer, Sharon Hamell, investigated financing options. ACI Computer offered both finance and operating leases at 10 percent for four years. Century was willing to match these terms for a finance lease but was not competitive with its rates on an operating lease. Next, she tried the firm's New York bank, but learned that their interest rate was three–quarters of a point higher. They did offer to get a proposal out from their lease subsidiary, which belatedly arrived just yesterday. She of course would include it in her part of the analysis if it was competitive. And finally, the company could pay cash, but that would take a little time to arrange since the company did not have an extra $3–$4 million of cash just lying around.

The details of the costs and financing terms for the ACI and Century systems are in EXHIBITS 2 and 3, respectively. It should be noted that if the company decides in favor of purchasing the new ACI computer, a $700,000 trade–in allowance would be given for the old ACI machine. The current street value on this system is only about $300,000, and will have a tax basis at year–end, when this transaction would be finalized, of $963,000. And finally, for analysis purposes, insurance is 0.5 percent of book value, personal property tax, 2.0 percent, sales tax is 5 percent, and federal and state income taxes combine to a 40 percent rate.

Best Choice

The decision on a new computer system will be made by Jack Johanek himself, after listening to the pros and cons on the two systems from Dennis Stanton and the financing options from Sharon Hamell. In making this decision, however, he wasn't willing to dismiss entirely the possibility of just paying a computer service firm to fill this need. In any event, the time to decide was now (actually a week from now), since a multi–million dollar marketing and business development campaign would commence soon, heralding Johanek Corporation as one of the largest, full–service housing and financial services specialists in the South.

Discussion Questions

1. What factors other than the economics of this decision need to be considered here? What option do they suggest?

2. What is the difference between trading in an old system and selling it outright?

3. Which system/financing option is the least cost alternative?

4. How much could the company pay to a computer service firm, on a levelized basis over a four–year period, for their computing needs?

5. What are the downside risks, if any, in this decision?

6. What is the best choice here, and why?

7. What additional information would be useful for this analysis?

Exhibit 1
Johanek Corporation
Revenues and Earnings
1986–1993

	1986	1987	1988	1989	1990	1991	1992	1993
Operating Revenues	223	330	381	437	338	323	426	567
Net Income	13	23	28	28	14	14	29	37

Exhibit 2
ACI Cost/Financing Specifics

COMPUTER: ACI Computer, AC 1170

FINANCING OPTION: Financed Purchase

> System Cost – $3,170,000
> System Software Installation and Support – $24,000
> Maintenance – $130,000 in year 1, 5 percent escalation/year thereafter
> Financing – 10 percent, 4–year level payment loan
> Residual Value – 16 percent

FINANCING OPTION: Bank Operating Lease

> Lease Payment – $600,000 per year, includes credit for old machine

FINANCING OPTION: Cash

> Assumptions same as financed purchase option except for Financing,
> which of course is cash.

Exhibit 3
Century Cost/Financing Specifics

COMPUTER: Century Information Systems, Century 9010

FINANCING OPTION: Financed Purchase

System Cost – $2,850,000
System Software Installation and Support – $24,000
Cooling System – $30,000
Maintenance – $150,000 for years 1–4
Financing – 10 percent, 4–year level payment loan
Residual Value – 16 percent

FINANCING OPTION: Operating Lease

Commitment Fee – 1 percent
Lease Payment – $800,000 per year
Lease Scheduled Value – .215 EOY 4, payment for the difference

Part V
Valuation

Case 13
Dahlberg's, Inc.

"Everything looks good." That was the word from Virginia Givens, vice–president of finance for Dahlberg's, as she passed Jim Dwyer, the company's CEO, on her way to her office. "Give me a few minutes, and I'll be right down." She had just returned from the "Big Apple" with the results of her negotiations with the company's banks and investment advisors. The bank credit facility was tentatively agreed upon. The commercial paper issue was assured. And the terms for permanent financing were discussed and detailed for the company's consideration.

That was the essence of Ms. Given's report, as she laid out the details and options for how the company could finance the acquisition of Garratt Companies. The next step, of course, was the formal negotiations with the senior executives of Garratt Companies. This would require a little sharpening of the pencil, both in determining what the firm was truly worth and what specific strategies the company should employ in approaching this rather unique organization.

Dahlberg's History

Dahlberg's is a national food wholesaler and regional retailer in general merchandise and food store sales. As recently as the late seventies, the retail business was still the primary profit generator, with roughly equal contributions from the department stores and grocery outlets. But by 1983, the food wholesale business had surpassed the company's retail activities and had driven its profitable operations ever since. In 1986 and 1987 in particular, Dahlberg's made several important acquisitions which thrust it into the big time for food wholesaling. Retailing, however, still accounts for some 30 percent of profits, primarily from supermarkets it operates under franchise from Cub Foods and a number of other food companies.

In addition, as a wholesaler to principally independent food stores, it provides dozens of support services to affiliated stores in over 30 states, from design and construction to marketing, management, and even some financial services, such as insurance and construction loans. These activities basically pay their way but are offered more out of necessity than as a profit center.

Essentially, the company has participated in the national growth of the industry as well as benefiting from the inevitable consolidation that has been occurring for more than a decade (see EXHIBITS 1 and 2). Other than the 1986 and 1987 acquisitions, Dahlberg's has made just modest additions, and a few subtractions, as opportunities and profit considerations dictated. The result has been a gradual rise into the top tier of their industry, which they now share with several large, privately held concerns.

Principally because of the size of the deal, the current effort to acquire Garratt represents a departure from past practice, and could be characterized as a merger as much as an acquisition.

Sources: Data and information based on various publications including S&P Stock Reports, S&P Industry Surveys.

Food Wholesaling Industry

Clearly, consolidation is one way to describe how the food wholesaling industry has developed in recent years, yet this does not adequately characterize the current dynamics. Credit analysts typically cite greater "operating risk" in recent assessments of the food wholesaling industry. The factors most often mentioned in these reviews are food price deflation, weak consumer spending, and heightened competition among food retailers. This is still a highly territorial business, so strong regional wholesalers (and retailers) are as much a threat as the large and ever–growing national organizations.

While this properly describes the wholesaling industry for the next few years, food wholesalers are by no means the monolithic entities they once were. In other words, not only is the food wholesaling industry changing, but the food wholesaling industry is not the only industry food wholesalers are in. Opportunities abound in the distribution system of this industry, and adept companies are finding profitable ways to exploit these opportunities.

Garratt Companies

Garratt Companies is about one–third the size of Dahlberg's (see EXHIBITS 3 and 4) and considerably more diverse. Food wholesaling is its primary business activity but it also operates numerous retail chain businesses in food, drugs, and general merchandise. Its wholesale activities include housewares, school supplies, health and beauty aids, bakery products and videotapes, as well as food products. It has similar types of real estate development and financial services as Dahlberg's but additionally provides lending services for fixtures, equipment and store improvements, leasing, and highly profitable data processing and management information systems services.

Geographically, Garratt Companies complements Dahlberg's quite nicely. Dahlberg's operates primarily in the Northwest and Midwest states, and through acquisition in the mid–eighties, in Florida and Georgia. Garratt's operations are primarily in New England and the Mid–Atlantic states, with a recent acquisition of a major southern retailer/wholesaler.

This highly diverse company does make it unusual in this industry, but what makes it truly unique is that it is, for all intents and purposes, an all–female owned and managed firm. Carol Stewart, Garratt's CEO, and a small group of the company's senior (female) management own about 31 percent of the total shares of stock outstanding. Ms. Stewart herself has been at the helm of Garratt Companies for the better part of the last 20 years, and over that time has been everything—"Entrepreneur of the Year," "Business Woman of the Year" (three times), "Small Business Person of the 80s," etc., and the firm has been cited as "Best Growth Company," "Wholesaler of the Year" (numerous times), and various "Bests" in a number of service and product line development areas in its industry.

The company is for sale. In order to continue to prosper in this industry and to achieve the profit potential the company believes is possible but has been unable to accomplish by itself, it engaged an investment advisor recently to help find a partner. Regarding the possible acquisition of Garratt Companies by Dahlberg's, the two have had brief discussions about this several months ago. They have limited knowledge of one another otherwise, although Garratt's bakery products subsidiary has actually been a supplier to Dahlberg's for many years.

The Offer

After going over the financing arrangements with Ms. Givens, Jim Dwyer called in his secretary to arrange an early morning meeting on Friday with the Executive Committee to review the position of the company on this acquisition and to finalize the negotiating strategy. In particular, he wanted to satisfy himself that the assumptions made in the valuation of Garratt were proper (see EXHIBITS 5 and 6).

A key assumption was, of course, the projected growth rate in sales. The 7–8 percent rate used in the valuation seemed right to him, in spite of industry forecasts of only 5 percent. The 1–1.5 percent used for the operating margin was consistent with the company's experience, but he couldn't help but notice how different this was from the rest of the industry. The assumption for capital spending, based on its historic relationship with sales, was surely too low since both companies were at capacity, and the very purpose of this acquisition was to take advantage of expansion opportunities. Depreciation expense based on the previous year's fixed assets seemed reasonable. And the cost of capital, derived from the required return on equity and a 9.5 percent cost of new "A+" rated debentures, which was just confirmed by Ms. Givens, was on target, although he noted that no final decision had been made on the target capital structure.

A little additional analysis was necessary in his view, but even assuming he had a more refined valuation, he wondered: What should the offer be?

Discussion Questions

1. What factors should be considered in mergers/acquisitions? What are the determinants of successful mergers/acquisitions?

2. For the purposes of valuation, project Garratt Companies' free cash flows. How will they be affected, if at all, if the two companies are combined?

3. What should be the discount rate? Why?

4. Estimate the value of Garratt Companies. What is the best approach to corporate valuation? What explicit or implicit assumptions have been made?

5. How should the acquisition of Garratt be financed? Or, more specifically, what should be the debt/equity mix?

6. Show what the combined firms would look like. What does an analysis of the projected financial statements reveal?

7. What should be the strategy for a successful acquisition? In other words, how should Dahlberg's approach Garratt, how much should they offer for the company, and what should be their negotiating tactics, etc.?

8. What additional information would be useful for this analysis?

Exhibit 1
Dahlberg's, Inc.
Statement of Operations, 1987–1991

($ mm)	1987	1988	1989	1990	1991
Revenues	9,066	9,372	10,296	11,136	11,612
– Operating Expenses	8,749	9,026	9,905	10,717	11,169
Operating Income	317	346	391	419	443
– Depreciation	92	110	118	131	137
+ Other Income	14	25	24	35	29
EBIT	239	261	297	323	335
– Interest Expense	54	63	73	80	81
Earnings Before Taxes	185	198	224	243	254
– Income Taxes	96	86	89	95	99
NET INCOME	89	112	135	148	155
CAPITAL EXPENDITURES	273	239	293	223	262

Exhibit 2
Dahlberg's, Inc.
Statement of Financial Condition, 1987–1991

($ mm)	1987	1988	1989	1990	1991
Assets					
Cash	3	2	2	2	3
Other Current Assets	852	930	1,043	1,079	1,141
Total Current Assets	855	932	1,045	1,081	1,144
Fixed Assets & Other	943	1,084	1,260	1,348	1,471
TOTAL ASSETS	1,798	2,016	2,305	2,429	2,615
Liabilities and Equity					
Total Current Liabilities	742	757	906	951	998
Other Long–Term Liabilities	4	2	4	5	26
Long–Term Debt	429	545	571	561	577
Preferred Stock	27	35	46	42	35
Common Equity	596	677	778	870	979
Total Invested Capital	1,052	1,257	1,395	1,473	1,591
TOTAL LIABILITIES AND EQUITY	1,798	2,016	2,305	2,429	2,615

Exhibit 3
Garratt Companies
Statement of Operations, 1987–1991

($ mm)	1987	1988	1989	1990	1991
Revenues	3,842	4,156	4,918	5,292	5,667
– Operating Expenses	3,775	4,090	4,861	5,240	5,605
Operating Income	67	66	57	52	62
– Depreciation	28	32	36	38	41
+ Other Income	41	51	84	96	103
EBIT	80	85	105	110	124
– Interest Expense	17	21	33	34	41
Earnings Before Taxes	63	64	72	76	83
– Income Taxes	28	25	29	29	32
NET INCOME	35	39	43	47	51
CAPITAL EXPENDITURES	64	72	88	89	120

Exhibit 4
Garratt Companies
Statement of Financial Condition, 1987–1991

($ mm)	1987	1988	1989	1990	1991
Assets					
Cash	32	39	9	2	11
Other Current Assets	337	412	476	521	573
Total Current Assets	369	451	485	523	584
Fixed Assets & Other	314	348	467	507	576
TOTAL ASSETS	683	799	952	1,030	1,160
Liabilities and Equity					
Total Current Liabilities	258	329	389	451	438
Other Long–Term Liabilities	5	16	34	37	32
Long–Term Debt	191	221	283	323	441
Preferred Stock	19	19	16	12	24
Common Equity	210	214	230	207	225
Total Invested Capital	420	454	529	542	690
TOTAL LIABILITIES AND EQUITY	683	799	952	1,030	1,160

Exhibit 5
Stock Market Data
Dahlberg's, Garratt, and Industry, 1986–1991

	1986	1987	1988	1989	1990	1991
Dahlberg's (Beta .81)						
Book Value	7.20	8.00	9.07	10.39	11.59	13.01
Earnings/Share	1.23	1.20	1.50	1.81	1.97	2.06
Dividends/Share	.37	.41	.44	.49	.59	.65
Avg. Mkt. Price	19.50	23.75	23.25	21.75	26.50	25.50
Price/Earnings	16	20	16	12	13	12
Garratt (Beta .94)						
Book Value	7.77	7.22	7.08	7.77	7.44	8.25
Earnings/Share	1.45	1.41	1.58	1.82	2.00	2.23
Dividends/Share	.48	.51	.52	.55	.59	.63
Avg. Mkt. Price	16.25	19.75	21.25	21.75	27.25	30.00
Price/Earnings	11	14	13	12	14	13
Industry (Beta 1.04)						
Market/Book	1.8	2.0	1.8	2.0	1.6	1.9
Price/Earnings	19	14	13	14	14	16

Exhibit 6
Industry Norms
Liquidity, Activity, Leverage, and Profitability
Ratios, 1987–1991

	1987	1988	1989	1990	1991
Current Ratio	1.6	1.4	1.7	1.5	1.5
Sales/NWC	23.9	31.2	26.4	31.2	27.5
Sales/Assets	5.5	4.7	4.7	5.0	4.6
Debt/Assets	.61	.61	.57	.55	.58
Debt/Capital	.46	.41	.39	.39	.40
Operating Margin %	2.2	2.2	2.3	2.7	2.7
Pretax Margin %	1.6	1.5	1.4	1.6	1.3
Pretax ROA %	9.2	8.0	6.9	7.4	6.6
Pretax ROE %	23	19	20	22	15

Case 14
Potawatomi Paper Company

The competition has been brutal in the paper industry the last couple of years and 1992 doesn't look like it will be much better. When the economy is weak, printed advertising declines, as does printed promotions and other business paper use. But some firms are making money, and Ron Melcher believes that Potawatomi Paper Company could be one of them. Melcher is a principal in Ashcroft Melcher, a regional investment banking firm which specializes in leveraged buyouts. It is flush with cash and would like to take the company private. If he is right that Potawatomi Paper is underperforming, a turnaround could yield tremendous profits in just a few short years—the goal being to "cash out" with a public offering at that time.

Potawatomi Paper

As one of the larger producers of newsprint in North America, Potawatomi Paper has sales and earnings that vary closely with the cyclical fluctuations of the industry to which it belongs. And the paper industry, although nondurable in nature, is a highly cyclical industry, and therefore in turn varies with the overall business cycle. Unfortunately, the weak recovery of the U.S. economy has dampened sales and held down prices of paper products for more than two years. As the first quarter of 1992 has developed, the economy remains sluggish and Potawatomi's sales generally reflect this weakness. The company is currently projecting only to break even this year, and could suffer a serious loss if it should lose a major mail order catalog job, which is a real possibility. The company's stock is trading at around $23 a share, a little below book value, or approximately $920 million in total capitalized value. But with continued poor earnings performances, the cost to acquire the company could be as much as $100 million less.

One perspective of what Ashcroft Melcher would be getting here lies in the comparative earnings and dividends streams of Potawatomi vs. the industry, and the market multiples of earnings and book values, provided in EXHIBIT 1. As the data illustrate, Potawatomi is not the only company having a tough time. But again, some firms are profitable in an currently weak industry.

Another perspective is in the assets themselves that would come with this deal. The company operates three large saw mills in the U.S. and Canada, and manufacturers pulp and paper products at major facilities in Nova Scotia, northern Wisconsin, Tennessee, and South Carolina. In addition, it just completed a new recycling plant in Georgia. Its mills are fully integrated and supplied by more than four million acres of timberlands. Potawatomi also operates eight plants throughout the United States which make nothing but continuous stock computer forms. And with its largest selling product, newsprint, it produces a fourth of its total output through joint venture agreements with publishers and printers. Finally, there are literally thousands of pieces of miscellaneous equipment, whose replacement cost would be substantially above book value.

Sources: Data and information based on various publications, including S&P Stock Reports, S&P Industry Surveys, RMA Annual Statement Studies, S&P Bond Guide.

The problem right now is that there is significant overcapacity in the industry and without an export boom, some plants (and possibly some companies) will have to close. For the survivors then, the upside potential in this industry could be quite impressive.

A third perspective is in the company's financial statements, as they have recorded the results of operations and the flow of funds into and out of the firm. These are provided in EXHIBITS 2 and 3, and they show quite clearly what a struggle it has been recently. Industry norms for the pulp and paper industry are shown in EXHIBIT 4.

Financing the Acquisition

Ron Melcher is convinced of the strategic value of this investment, although the actual price still needs to be determined. Even given this, a major question that remains is how the acquisition will be financed. As indicated earlier, the company has plenty of cash and is well connected to institutional lenders, so the issue is not sources of funds, but rather what the optimal mix of debt and equity should be.

As a guide in assessing the nature of financial leverage and its presence in the paper industry, the capital structures of the industry participants and their respective bond ratings are provided in EXHIBIT 5. Also, the historical rates on long–term debt of varying degrees of risk are summarized in EXHIBIT 6. It should be noted that this industry employs long–term leasing to a much greater extent than most others. But the implicit rates in these contracts are similar to what would be charged under similar termed debt contracts.

Mr. Melcher's expert on the issue of capital structure is Jack Kauffman, the highly credentialed financial economist "on leave" from his faculty post, to which he may never be able to afford to return. This was always an interesting theoretical question, but now he is expected to practice what he formerly used to preach. In addition to prescribing what the specific mix should be in this particular situation, Mr. Melcher asked for an analysis of the impact of this decision on earnings per share in 1994, assuming growth in operating income of 8–15 percent per year for the years 1993 and 1994.

Discussion Questions

1. If Ashcroft Melcher believes the company is undervalued, why doesn't it just purchase the stock and resell it at a profit later?

2. Determine an approximate acquisition value of the company's equity assuming losses mount to $100 million in 1992.

3. From the data on industry competitors, illustrate how cost of capital varies with capital structure.

4. Analyze Potawatomi's current capital structure and what would be its "optimal" structure.

5. Does the choice of capital structure affect the price Ashcroft Melcher should pay for the firm?

6. What is the significance and impact of the uncertainty in the projected income estimates?

7. How much should be paid to acquire this company, and how should it be financed?

8. What additional information would be useful for this analysis?

Exhibit 1
Earnings per Share, Payout, Book Value per Share, and Market Price
Pulp and Paper Industry Participants
1987–1991

	Earnings/Share					Payout				
	87	88	89	90	91	87	88	89	90	91
POTAWATOMI	2.13	4.37	3.66	2.30	1.15	39	22	30	52	104
Abitibi Price	1.31	2.18	0.60	(0.59)	(0.97)	34	37	140	n/m	n/m
Boise Cascade	3.70	6.34	6.19	1.62	(2.46)	31	21	23	94	n/m
Champion Int'l.	4.03	4.80	4.56	2.11	0.14	18	20	24	52	179
Chesapeake	1.47	2.51	2.31	0.81	0.75	31	20	29	89	96
Consolidated	2.20	3.44	3.85	3.27	2.10	36	28	30	39	61
Domtar Inc.	1.30	0.94	0.03	(3.34)	(1.46)	28	42	n/m	n/m	n/m
Federal Paper	1.86	3.51	5.00	2.74	1.83	22	18	19	37	55
Georgia–Pacific	4.23	4.76	7.42	4.28	(0.92)	25	26	20	37	n/m
Glatfelter	2.25	3.40	3.85	3.76	3.34	24	21	26	29	36
Int'l. Paper	3.68	6.57	7.72	5.21	3.61	33	19	20	32	47
James River	2.36	2.87	2.45	0.66	0.66	17	17	24	91	106
Kimberly–Clark	1.87	2.36	2.63	2.70	3.18	39	34	49	50	48
Longview Fibre	1.17	1.74	1.21	1.13	0.32	27	23	40	46	163
Louisiana–Pacif.	3.27	3.54	5.04	2.46	1.55	24	25	19	42	70
Macmillan Bldl.	1.97	2.58	1.96	0.32	(0.85)	31	28	35	213	n/m
Mead Corp.	3.47	5.54	3.33	1.71	1.29	19	13	26	57	78
Pope & Talbot	2.33	2.68	3.70	1.70	(0.44)	19	19	16	42	n/m
Potlatch Corp.	3.13	4.04	4.79	3.41	1.92	27	24	23	36	70
Scott Paper	3.06	5.23	5.11	2.01	(0.95)	22	14	16	40	n/m
Sonoco Products	1.40	2.20	2.36	1.16	2.20	36	29	34	78	42
Stone Container	2.81	5.69	4.76	1.59	(0.79)	9	6	15	45	n/m
Temple–Inland	2.35	3.58	3.75	4.20	2.51	15	12	15	19	35
Union Camp	2.83	4.25	4.35	3.35	1.80	40	29	33	46	87
Westvaco Corp.	2.25	3.10	3.45	2.90	2.10	31	27	27	35	51
Weyerhauser	2.12	2.68	1.56	1.87	(0.50)	42	43	77	64	n/m
Williamette	4.78	6.34	7.52	5.10	1.80	23	19	19	33	89

Exhibit 1 (cont.)

	Book Value/Share					Market Price				
	87	**88**	**89**	**90**	**91**	**87**	**88**	**89**	**90**	**91**
POTAWATOMI	17.6	21.1	23.4	24.4	24.4	33.3	31.1	29.9	22.3	24.5
Abitibi Price	11.9	13.9	14.2	13.2	11.9	21.7	18.6	14.8	12.1	12.3
Boise Cascade	32.4	37.3	33.5	33.5	30.2	40.5	43.0	43.9	33.0	23.8
Champion Int'l.	30.8	35.1	38.6	39.6	39.5	33.9	33.8	33.3	28.4	26.4
Chesapeake	10.0	12.1	13.5	13.6	13.8	20.4	19.1	21.0	17.1	18.6
Consolidated	14.0	16.5	19.1	21.1	22.0	30.0	35.6	39.0	38.0	37.0
Domtar Inc.	8.4	10.7	10.8	7.5	6.2	13.6	11.0	12.9	9.5	7.3
Federal Paper	13.4	16.3	18.4	18.9	19.5	19.0	19.2	24.8	20.3	25.1
Georgia–Pacific	25.6	27.8	30.3	10.8	9.0	37.8	36.8	49.3	38.8	48.3
Glatfelter	11.5	14.0	16.3	18.3	20.0	30.6	33.6	43.0	39.2	50.2
Int'l. Paper	34.8	38.4	43.0	45.1	43.7	42.4	42.9	51.9	51.3	64.4
James River	20.4	22.5	24.7	25.0	24.8	31.1	25.4	30.1	23.9	23.1
Kimberly–Clark	9.8	11.6	12.9	14.1	15.7	25.7	28.0	33.2	36.8	45.1
Longview Fibre	5.1	6.4	7.1	7.5	7.3	10.5	12.0	14.4	11.2	12.5
Louisiana–Pacif.	27.2	30.5	31.0	32.5	33.4	30.6	31.5	35.7	32.8	36.4
Macmillan Bldl.	9.0	11.2	12.7	12.4	11.6	17.0	16.0	16.2	14.2	16.8
Mead Corp.	17.2	24.0	21.0	21.8	21.2	34.7	39.3	40.4	29.5	30.9
Pope & Talbot	11.0	13.3	16.5	17.4	15.7	18.5	19.3	23.8	18.9	15.9
Potlatch Corp.	21.9	25.0	28.7	30.9	31.5	31.4	29.2	34.7	33.8	37.4
Scott Paper	21.4	26.5	28.0	29.5	26.9	35.5	37.6	45.4	40.7	38.1
Sonoco Products	7.7	9.3	10.0	10.6	11.6	24.4	27.3	35.8	31.8	33.6
Stone Container	12.4	17.7	4.3	5.0	5.9	27.6	30.1	29.3	16.7	17.5
Temple–Inland	16.8	19.4	22.0	26.4	27.9	25.9	24.2	29.4	31.4	40.0
Union Camp	20.2	22.7	25.2	27.8	27.4	37.1	34.7	37.4	35.1	43.1
Westvaco Corp.	18.2	20.4	22.9	24.8	25.8	30.3	28.1	30.1	26.8	32.7
Weyerhauser	18.2	19.8	20.2	19.2	17.3	30.0	26.3	28.6	22.9	25.4
Williamette	24.2	29.4	35.4	38.8	39.0	47.4	46.0	48.3	43.6	49.8

Exhibit 2
Statements of Operations
1987–1991

($mm) Year Ended December 31	1987	1988	1989	1990	1991
Revenues	1,231	1,140	1,450	1,380	1,289
– Operating Expenses	927	978	1,063	1,088	1,053
Operating Income	304	432	387	292	236
– Depreciation	85	98	107	117	132
EBIT	219	334	280	175	104
– Interest Expense	47	36	44	47	46
Earnings Before Taxes	172	298	236	128	58
+ Other Income	5	4	25	13	11
Net Before Taxes	177	302	261	141	69
– Income Taxes	96	138	116	54	23
NET INCOME	81	164	145	87	46

Exhibit 3
Statements of Financial Condition
1987–1991

($mm) Year Ended December 31	1987	1988	1989	1990	1991
Assets					
Cash	33	25	92	18	28
Other Current Assets	234	263	265	265	358
Total Current Assets	267	288	357	283	386
Long–Term Assets	1,433	1,592	1,927	2,015	2,394
TOTAL ASSETS	1,700	1,880	2,284	2,298	2,780
Liabilities and Equity					
Total Current Liabilities	161	220	246	223	282
Other Long–Term Liabilities	7	8	8	7	70
Long–Term Debt	350	274	504	488	840
Other Long–Term Capital	469	551	619	645	645
Common Equity	713	827	907	935	943
Total Invested Capital	1,532	1,652	2,030	2,068	2,428
TOTAL LIABILITIES AND EQUITY	1,700	1,880	2,284	2,298	2,780

Exhibit 4
Industry Financial Ratios
1987–1991

	1987	1988	1989	1990	1991
Current Ratio	1.5	1.9	1.6	1.7	1.6
Cash Ratio	0.16	0.19	0.20	0.21	0.22
Sales/Net	6.2	7.6	5.5	5.6	4.6
Fixed Assets	2.0	2.4	2.0	2.2	1.8
Debt to Total Assets	60.5	60.2	60.7	58.2	60.5
EBIT/Interest	3.2	4.6	3.5	2.7	3.2
Pretax Margin on Sales	4.3%	5.0%	4.9%	5.1%	4.5%
Pretax Return on Assets	7.1%	9.3%	6.8%	6.6%	6.7%
Pretax Return on Equity	20.5%	25.2%	21.2%	17.0%	17.3%

Exhibit 5
Capital Structure and Bond Ratings
Pulp and Paper Industry Participants
1987–1991

	Equity/Capital (%)					S&P Bond Rating
	1987	1988	1989	1990	1991	
POTAWATOMI	47	50	45	45	39	BBB+
Abitibi Price	50	53	56	57	57	–
Boise Cascade	53	59	38	33	29	BBB
Champion Int'l.	56	58	55	50	48	BBB
Chesapeake	45	47	45	40	39	BBB–
Consolidated	83	83	84	84	73	–
Domtar Inc.	46	45	45	36	32	–
Federal Paper	37	43	40	34	35	BBB–
Georgia–Pacific	57	44	46	33	38	BB+
Glatfelter	53	76	85	84	85	–
Int'l. Paper	58	60	61	57	57	A–
James River	45	43	45	46	46	BBB+
Kimberly–Clark	54	57	58	61	61	AA
Longview Fibre	62	65	60	51	46	–
Louisiana–Pacif.	60	70	64	62	66	–
Macmillan Bldl.	55	60	54	48	46	–
Mead Corp.	56	56	57	50	49	BBB+
Pope & Talbot	69	63	69	69	70	–
Potlatch Corp.	50	53	55	60	54	A–
Scott Paper	53	50	48	42	42	BBB+
Sonoco Products	54	58	63	59	71	A+
Stone Container	38	54	26	27	26	B+
Temple–Inland	59	61	41	60	54	A
Union Camp	44	40	39	64	70	A+
Westvaco Corp.	60	59	56	53	54	A
Weyerhaeuser	55	41	44	39	41	A+
Williamette	60	59	63	57	52	A

Exhibit 6
Historical Interest Rates by S&P Bond Ratings
(1987–1992)

	AAA	AA	A	BBB	BB	B
1987	9.6%	10.0%	10.2%	10.8%	–	–
1988	9.5	9.9	10.4	10.8	11.2%	12.2%
1989	9.3	9.6	10.1	10.5	11.8	12.9
1990	9.3	9.6	10.0	10.8	13.0	16.8
1991	8.6	8.9	9.4	10.5	11.7	16.7
1992e	8.4	8.6	9.1	9.3	11.2	12.1

Case 15
Cognoscere Corporation

The future course of the computer industry remains a mystery, even for such visionaries as Peter Tabor, Cognoscere's executive vice–president for development. Broad themes and technological possibilities can be pondered, but from a business perspective, it is hard to forecast the pace of development, what direction is implied by the industry's lurches from one concept or "standard" to another, the nature and lag of the marketplace in productively adapting evolving technology, and more recently, who will be teaming up with whom, in terms of both supply and demand. One thing that is clear, however, is that businesses and governments rely increasingly on information, and that the information comes in all forms and from numerous, ever diverse, sources.

For all the distractions of hardware and software particulars, to Peter Tabor the industry has been fundamentally an information industry, up to this point. From a business perspective, he has put his company in a position to cash in on this, but now he is beginning to see the industry move on from this information age to an age of discovery. Businesses and governments now seem destined to harness this great power for advances of truly epic proportions in the sciences of health and the environment and the business of global economics. The significance of this for Mr. Tabor's software services company is that he needs to push his firm more strongly and rapidly in the direction of the commercialization of science. In essence, this would allow the great thinking machines of today to process vast amounts of diverse information, in a scientific setting, for solutions to some of life's greatest unknowns.

To this end, the work of colleague Susan Schaefer, a software engineer at Scientific Systems Corporation, has captivated Peter Tabor's attention in recent months. Like his own company, Scientific Systems designs, develops, markets, and supports an integrated line of computer–aided software engineering (CASE) products for the development of complex computer–based information and analysis systems. But unlike Cognoscere Corporation, these powerful programming tools are expressly written for the scientific community; scientists can study science, rather than spending months or years developing the complex code necessary to engage in scientific research and discovery.

Scientific Systems Corporation

The company Ms. Schaefer works for is less than five years old and was spun off by the Antone Institute, a prestigious Washington State biotech research organization, to allow for the commercial development of its computer software capabilities. It has doubled its sales each year since its inception, reaching $124 million in 1991, and now has almost 500 employees. Its stock is traded over the counter but is closely held by the company's five directors, a West Coast investment bank, a handful of other institutional investors, and its employees. There are 100 million shares authorized but only 12.5 million outstanding. Its impressive financial performance is shown in EXHIBITS 1 and 2. EXHIBIT 3 contains some per share and market data.

Sources: Data and information based on various publications including S&P Stock Reports, S&P Industry Surveys.

But success is never assured. The recent release of the newest version of its bread and butter CASE series of products contained some serious bugs, which slowed revenues and increased costs. Results from 1992 are expected to show a drop–off in sales of 7–8 percent, operating expenses at 93 percent of sales and zero profit, for all intents and purposes. The problem the company is beginning to experience is the myriad hosts and configurations that it must adapt its software to, if it expects to grow. This adaptation is one of the real strengths of Cognoscere Corporation; it has adapted its CASE tools to over 450 different models of computers by 85 different manufacturers. In fact, this is rather unique for a company in this industry and represents a true competitive advantage.

Cognoscere Corporation

Cognoscere has strong database products and has been a big UNIX player for many years. Its software runs mainly on midrange computers, but it does have solid PC offerings, giving it excellent network potential. All of its products are based on Structured Query Language (SQL), an industry standard created by IBM. Essentially, its software is a fourth generation application development language which consolidates SQL with syntax for menu creation, formatted screen generation, and report writing.

Approximately 35 percent of sales are the result of distribution agreements with partners in Europe and Japan. And its current joint venture with a Fortune 50 computer manufacturer for CASE programs promises to yield both great technology and widespread distribution of its products.

Cognoscere Corporation was incorporated in 1986, has 1,100 employees currently, and reached $145 million in sales in 1989. About half of its growth has been internally generated and half generated through acquisition of smaller software companies. In 1990 it also stumbled, with weak sales, ineffective cost controls, and an accounting change brought on by a legal suit which effectively reduced reported revenues. Fortunately, the first half of 1991 has shown strong international sales and increased operating efficiency, and should return the company to profitability and 25 percent revenue growth.

Cognoscere's recent financial performance is given in EXHIBITS 4 and 5, with per share and market data in EXHIBIT 3, along with Scientific System's. Approximately 13 million shares of common stock are outstanding, with 25 million authorized.

Possibility of a Merger

Cognoscere is always looking for possible acquisitions—of competitors, in order to gain size, and of emerging technologies, to flatten its learning curve. It also has had success with joint ventures, with both marketing agreements and, most recently, with a joint development pact.

It was in this spirit that Alex Hernandez, Cognoscere's CEO, followed Peter Tabor's suggestion to contact Scientific Systems about a possible business combination. After several rounds of discussions, a merger was agreed to in principle, taking the form of an exchange of stock. It was decided that all products would be cross licensed, all employees would be retained, and Cognoscere would be the surviving entity. The conversion rate between the two companies, however, remained in dispute. This is not entirely unexpected, given the wide range of assessments of software companies by the market (see EXHIBIT 6). But as a possible solution to the discordance, the two companies agreed to hire a neutral, mutually acceptable, investment advisor to estimate values.

Discussion Questions

1. Estimate what each of the companies is currently worth.

2. Analyze the potential for dilution and appreciation by showing the two companies' 1991 earnings, earnings per share, price/earnings ratios, and market prices, separately, and then combined.

3. What effect would the merger have on market values? Use P/E ratios as a framework for analyzing this.

4. Acquisition terms are generally affected by earnings and earnings growth, dividends, market and book values, and net current assets. Analyze the potential impact of each of these on the terms of this acquisition.

5. Discuss the qualitative issues which will drive the numbers if these two firms are combined. Estimate what incremental value, if any, is attributable to synergy.

6. What should the exchange ratio be between the two companies' stocks? Why?

7. What additional information would be useful for this analysis?

Exhibit 1
Scientific Systems Corporation
Statement of Operations, 1988–1991

($mm) Years Ending June 30	1988	1989	1990	1991
Revenues	14.0	33.0	66.2	124.3
– Operating Expenses	11.4	25.3	51.0	97.8
Operating Income	2.6	7.7	15.2	26.5
– Depreciation	0.6	1.4	2.9	5.0
+ Other Income	0.4	1.5	1.9	2.8
EBIT	2.4	7.8	14.2	24.3
– Interest Expense	–	–	–	–
Earnings Before Taxes	2.4	7.8	14.2	24.3
– Income Taxes	0.4	1.5	4.4	9.0
NET INCOME	2.0	6.3	9.8	15.3
CAPITAL EXPENDITURES	0.6	6.6	13.7	20.1

Exhibit 2
Scientific Systems Corporation
Statements of Financial Condition, 1988–1991

($mm) Years Ending June 30	1988	1989	1990	1991
Assets				
Cash	n/a	3.7	37.1	41.4
Other Current Assets	n/a	14.8	18.9	47.4
Total Current Assets	n/a	18.5	56.0	88.8
Fixed Assets & Other	n/a	5.2	16.0	31.1
TOTAL ASSETS	n/a	23.7	72.0	119.9
Liabilities and Equity				
Total Current Liabilities	n/a	12.4	19.9	45.0
Other Long–Term Liabilities	n/a	0.1	0.0	0.1
Long–Term Debt	n/a	0.5	0.0	0.0
Other Long–Term Capital	n/a	0.0	0.5	0.6
Common Equity	n/a	10.7	51.6	74.2
Total Invested Capital	n/a	11.2	52.1	74.8
TOTAL LIABILITIES AND EQUITY	n/a	23.7	72.0	119.9

Exhibit 3
Per Share and Market Data
Scientific Systems and Cognoscere
Corporation

Scientific Systems	1988	1989	1990	1991
Earnings/Share	.24	.74	.83	1.22
Dividends/Share	–	–	–	–
Price – High	–	17.125	27.500	43.250
– Low	–	13.250	10.000	10.500
Avg. Mkt. Price	–	15.188	18.750	26.875
Price/Earnings	–	21x	23x	22x

Cognoscere Corp.	1987	1988	1989	1990
Earnings/Share	.66	.03	.50	(1.82)
Dividends/Share	–	–	–	–
Price – High	31.250	25.750	15.375	17.500
– Low	10.000	6.625	7.625	3.500
Avg. Mkt. Price	20.625	16.188	11.500	10.500
Price/Earnings	31x	540x	23x	n/m

Exhibit 4
Cognoscere Corporation
Statement of Operations, 1987–1990

($mm) Years Ending December 31	1987	1988	1989	1990
Operating Revenues	42.0	104.5	145.0	146.0
– Operating Expenses	32.0	100.3	128.1	152.7
Operating Income	10.0	3.7	16.9	(6.7)
– Depreciation	1.0	4.0	6.3	7.5
+ Other Income	1.5	0.9	(0.5)	(8.5)
EBIT	10.5	0.6	10.1	(22.7)
– Interest Expense	–	–	–	–
Earnings Before Taxes	10.5	0.6	10.1	(22.7)
– Income Taxes	4.6	0.2	3.7	0.4
NET INCOME	5.9	0.4	6.4	(23.1)
CAPITAL EXPENDITURES	5.0	31.0	9.3	12.5

Exhibit 5
Cognoscere Corporation
Statement of Financial Condition, 1987–1990

($mm) Years Ending December 31	1987	1988	1989	1990
Assets				
Cash	31.5	27.8	25.2	20.5
Other Current Assets	16.5	55.2	81.8	48.5
Total Current Assets	48.0	83.0	107.0	69.0
Fixed Assets & Other	6.0	33.0	36.0	41.0
TOTAL ASSETS	54.0	116.0	143.0	110.0
Liabilities and Equity				
Total Current Liabilities	8.6	23.2	36.5	41.4
Other Long–Term Liabilities	(0.6)	(0.2)	0.5	0.6
Long–Term Debt	0.2	24.4	30.3	29.8
Other Long–Term Capital	1.2	2.2	1.7	0.1
Common Equity	44.6	66.4	74.0	38.1
Total Invested Capital	46.0	93.0	106.0	68.0
TOTAL LIABILITIES AND EQUITY	54.0	116.0	143.0	110.0

Exhibit 6
Equity Characteristics of Computer Software Companies
1990

Company	Average Price	Market to Book	Price/ Earnings	Growth*	Dividend Yield	Beta
Adobe Systems	$33.9	6.6	19	68.0%	0.6%	n/a
Aldus Corp.	23.3	2.8	14	38.1	–	n/a
Ashton–Tate	10.0	1.4	n/m	n/m	–	1.67
Autodesk	46.1	5.2	20	n/m	1.0	1.50
BMC Software	24.0	5.8	24	48.4	–	n/a
Boole & Babbage	16.3	2.2	n/m	67.1	–	n/a
Borland Int'l	21.3	3.8	12	n/m	–	n/a
Cadence Design	21.1	4.0	18	60.5	–	n/a
Computer Assc.	10.8	1.9	13	14.1	1.3	1.47
LEGENT	23.9	3.3	16	27.0	–	1.42
Lotus Development	25.9	3.5	48	(20.0)	–	1.54
Microsoft	40.9	7.8	27	54.3	–	1.47
Novell	11.9	4.2	18	52.0	–	1.50
Oracle Systems	17.7	6.0	21	92.6	–	1.86
Pansophic Systems	15.3	2.4	14	53.4	–	1.62
Software Publishing	20.0	2.7	13	61.8	–	1.82
System Software	20.8	4.8	15	67.2	1.1	n/a
Systems Center	14.7	10.3	n/m	n/m	–	2.07
Wordstar Int'l	1.1	0.7	n/m	n/m	–	1.31
Cognoscere Corp.	10.5[1]	3.7	n/m	n/m	–	1.91
Scientific Systems	18.8[2]	3.3	23	n/m	–	n/a

* 3–Year average annual growth in earnings.

[1] Recent price (9/91) of Cognoscere Corp. – 6.75.
[2] Recent price (9/91) of Scientific Systems – 12.50.

Case 16
Loeffler Tool, Inc.

This was a difficult call. James Allen, a regional investment banker in Philadelphia's Russell, Allen and Co., just couldn't get comfortable with the proposal he was about to present to the Executive Committee of Loeffler Tool and Machinery, the machine tools division of SSI of America, Inc. Although he had thoroughly investigated the machine tools industry, and the operations of the Loeffler division, he struggled to reconcile Loeffler's (and the industry's) weak performance over the last five years with the double–digit growth that was forecast for the next few years (see EXHIBIT 1). His leveraged buyout proposal hinged on this dramatic shift in industry and company fortunes, and both he (through his firm's investment) and the management of what would be Loeffler Tool, Inc., stood to make or lose a great deal of money on this gamble.

He kept staring at the financial projections on the spreadsheet in front of him, and then examined the neatly bound financing proposal he would be presenting tomorrow. Had he been too optimistic in his assessment of the division's prospects? Had he been too aggressive in "selling" this LBO idea to Loeffler's wantful but financially naive management? Had he biased his own view of the market's receptivity to this offering in his effort to make the deal work? And in the back of his mind, he also wondered whether Hanover Capital, the major creditor in this transaction, had similar doubts, but was banking on the sterling reputation of Russell, Allen and Co. Although not etched in stone, this proposal, if agreed upon in principle, would set in motion a very involved and expensive process of establishing the new Loeffler Tool, Inc.

Background

About a year ago, SSI of America, Inc., the U.S. unit of the French industrial conglomerate, made a strategic decision to divest itself of its minimally profitable and highly volatile machine tools division, Loeffler Tool and Machinery. With the industry still in the doldrums, and worldwide competition intensifying, especially from the Japanese (see EXHIBITS 1 and 2), SSI decided to redeploy its investment into the wide array of opportunities in the burgeoning "Europe 1992" market back home. Not surprisingly, it found little interest initially, but in the last six months it has received a couple of nibbles, one from a U.S. firm and one from a Canadian company. While trying to keep these possibilities moving forward, SSI has turned its attention to a recent proposition by Loeffler's senior management for a leveraged buyout. However, because of the volatile nature of the industry, and the limited amount of debt that could be used to finance such a purchase, it is more than a little curious about how such a deal would be structured. But to SSI, it simply boils down to whether the management group can come up with an offer that will be competitive.

Sources: Data and information based on various publications including S&P Stock Reports, S&P Industry Surveys, U.S. Industrial Outlook.

The Loeffler management group is headed by Frank Schubert, the unit's president, and includes Allan Hansen, executive vice–president and legal counsel, George Walinski, director of manufacturing/operations, Jean Schroeder, director of research and development, and Doug Shoults, division controller. After observing the cool response to SSI's initial efforts to sell the division, the five began talking with one another about an LBO, but based their assessment strictly on an operational knowledge of the business. Because of their profound ignorance of finance, they decided to hire a premier investment banking firm, Russell, Allen and Co., to advise them.

In Allen's initial analysis of the situation he concluded that selling the division to a large diversified industrial firm made the most sense. The unstable nature of the business could be diversified within such an entity, the resulting size would be a competitive advantage, and the capital needs in the future would be more easily arranged. This, of course, was not the answer the group was looking for, and after a couple of rounds of discussion, the second bringing Hanover Capital into the talks, James Allen indicated that a management leveraged buyout could be worked out.

Recent Financial Performance

Unlike others in the industry, Loeffler Tool and Machinery had been profitable in each of the last five years, although only marginally (see EXHIBIT 3). In addition to only modest growth, the feeble returns on equity have been due in part to a very conservative financial structure (see EXHIBIT 4). A leveraged buyout, of course, would solve that. The most vexing problem all along though has been the unpredictable behavior of the industry. Loeffler, for its part, has recognized where its own market has been heading and is now a successful producer of numerically controlled machine tools, as well as automated strip metal processing machinery. But the dynamics of this industry, and its rapid international development, gives pause for concern, even with well–managed operations.

The first half of 1989 has been very positive for both Loeffler and the industry. Sales are up, significant backlogs have developed, and exports are surging. Full year revenues are expected to be approximately 9 percent higher for the company (see EXHIBIT 5). And Loeffler's management is expecting to match industry forecasts of 10 percent per year in shipments for the next few years. Earnings growth should be even better, now that the division has developed a better handle on its operating expenses, thereby boosting its gross margin. In summary, the management of Loeffler Tool and Machinery believes that they have a solid basis, both operationally and financially, for launching a new firm—and into what should be a healthy machine tools industry, both domestically and abroad, in the years to come.

The Proposal

It was in this spirit that James Allen revised his outlook for a leveraged buyout. As he compared Loeffler to other publicly traded firms in the industry (see EXHIBIT 6), he began to see that it was a strong performer in what was undeniably a weak industry. With the industry projected to improve, the firm could have a very bright future.

Thus, assuming a market to book ratio for the equity of 1:1, Allen estimated that the division was worth approximately $85 million, and that $67 million in equity would have to be financed. Hanover Capital was willing to provide $13.375 million of financing at 13 percent (with $800,000 sinking fund payments in the first five years, $975,000 in years 6–15), each of the five principals in the new venture $225,000, Russell, Allen and Co. $2.5 million, and the rest would be raised in an initial public offering by year end. Investment banking fees are estimated to be about 5 percent, and legal and other expenses approximately $875,000.

The deal certainly looked feasible on paper. They always do. With this thought, Allen turned off the lights, locked up the office, and headed for home. A leisurely meal in a relaxing environment was all he wanted to think about at this point.

Discussion Questions

1. Under what circumstances are leveraged buyouts most likely to succeed? What factors contribute most to this success?

2. What sort of financial performance would you expect for this new firm over the next three years? Will cash flow be a problem?

3. Is the degree of financial leverage appropriate for this company? What effect would a 90/10, or 100/0 split in the equity/long–term debt ratio have on the firm? Is a greater debt proportion possible?

4. How will future capital requirements and net working capital needs be met for this firm?

5. At what price should the new issue be sold? What considerations should go into the establishment of an issue price? If the five managers are allowed to purchase their stock at $1 per share, how many shares will be issued? What is the book and market return for an investment in this company over the next three years?

6. Are there risks in underpricing or overpricing the stock to Russell, Allen and Co.? To Loeffler Tool, Inc.?

7. What would be your recommendation to SSI of America, Inc., regarding the disposition of Loeffler Tool and Machinery?

8. What additional information would be useful for this analysis?

Exhibit 1
Machine Tools Industry
Industry and Product Trends, 1984–1992

($ mm)	Actual					Est.	Projected		
	1984	1985	1986	1987	1988	1989	1990	1991	1992
Shipments									
Industry	4521	4790	4964	4658	4993	6170	6788	7441	8185
Product	4178	4354	4370	4042	4354	5463	6026	6605	7266
Imports	1663	2117	2693	2397	2476	3019	2661	2771	2886
Exports	744	778	914	1011	1226	1631	1920	2093	2282

Exhibit 2
Machine Tools Industry
Major Trading Partners, 1988

Exports		Imports	
Canada and Mexico	28.1%	Canada and Mexico	10.8%
South America	6.1	South America	0.4
European Community	21.1	European Community	18.9
East Asia NICs	15.5	East Asia NICs	7.7
Japan	7.9	Japan	49.7
Other	21.3	Other	12.5
Total	100.0%	Total	100.0%

Exhibit 3
Loeffler Tool and Machinery Division
Statement of Operations, 1984–1988

($ mm)	1984	1985	1986	1987	1988
Revenues	68.0	79.0	64.0	73.0	90.0
– Operating Expenses	62.5	73.8	61.5	71.1	86.2
Operating Income	5.5	5.2	2.5	1.9	3.8
– Depreciation	2.5	1.7	1.7	1.6	1.7
+ Other Income	2.1	1.6	1.3	1.1	1.1
EBIT	5.1	5.1	2.1	1.4	3.2
– Interest Expense	0.1	0.2	0.3	0.3	0.3
Earnings Before Taxes	5.0	4.9	1.8	1.1	2.9
– Income Taxes	2.5	2.2	0.7	0.6	1.1
NET INCOME	2.5	2.7	1.1	0.5	1.8
RETURN ON EQUITY	3.8%	4.0%	1.7%	0.1%	2.8%

Exhibit 4
Loeffler Tool and Machinery Division
Statement of Financial Condition, 1984–1988

($ mm)	1984	1985	1986	1987	1988
Assets					
Cash	16.5	14.2	12.4	14.4	12.6
Other Current Assets	45.2	48.3	50.2	51.5	55.9
Total Current Assets	61.7	62.5	62.6	65.9	68.5
Fixed Assets & Other	21.1	21.1	21.2	22.4	21.7
TOTAL ASSETS	82.8	83.6	83.8	88.3	90.2
Liabilities and Equity					
Total Current Liabilities	14.9	14.9	16.8	22.3	22.3
Other Long–Term Liabilities	–	–	–	–	–
Long–Term Debt	–	–	–	–	–
Other Long–Term Capital	1.3	1.3	1.3	1.1	4.3
Common Equity	66.6	67.4	65.7	64.9	63.6
Total Invested Capital	67.9	68.7	67.0	66.0	67.9
TOTAL LIABILITIES AND EQUITY	82.8	83.6	83.8	88.3	90.2

Exhibit 5
Loeffler Tool and Machinery Division
Estimated 1989 Statements

($mm) Statement of Financial Position		($mm) Statement of Operations	
Cash	6	Operating Revenues	98.0
Other Current Assets	57	−Operating Expenses	89.6
Total Current Assets	63	Operating Income	8.4
Fixed Assets & Other	22	−Depreciation	1.6
TOTAL ASSETS	85	+Other Income	0.9
Total Current Liabilities	18	EBIT	7.7
Other Long–Term Liabilities	−	−Interest Expense	0.3
Long–Term Debt	−	Earnings Before Taxes	7.4
Other Long–Term Capital	−	−Income Taxes	2.3
Common Equity	67	NET INCOME	5.1
Total Invested Capital	67		
TOTAL LIABILITIES AND EQUITY	85		

Exhibit 6
Machine Tools Industry Competitors
1988

	Loeffler	Acme–Clev.	Brown & Sharpe	Cincinnati Milacron	Cross & Trecker	Gleason
Assets	90.2	129	166	721	381	186
Common Equity	63.6	61	86	221	167	93
% of Long–Term Capital	98%	82%	75%	52%	81%	95%
Sales	90.0	176	181	858	428	211
Net Income	1.8	(30)	(3)	25	(23)	(4)
Margin	2.0%	n.a	1.9%	2.9%	n/a	n/a
ROA	2.0%	n.a	2.0%	2.6%	n/a	n/a
ROE	2.7%	n.a	3.8%	8.2%	n/a	n/a
Market/Book	–	1.09	0.80	2.42	1.19	0.79
Price/Earnings	–	n/a	21	21	n/a	n/a
Beta	–	.96	.68	1.32	1.07	0.84

	1983	1984	1985	1986	1987	1988	Growth
Sales ($ mm)							
Loeffler	59	68	79	64	73	90	8.8%
Acme–Clev.	173	213	221	186	177	176	0.3%
Brown & Sharpe	131	122	121	138	152	181	6.7%
Cinc.–Milacron	559	661	732	850	828	858	8.9%
Cross & Trecker	150	268	423	418	422	428	23.3%
Gleason	164	214	229	252	229	211	5.2%
Earnings/Share ($mm)							
Loeffler	0.5	2.5	2.7	1.1	0.5	1.8	29.2%
Acme–Clev.	(7.39)	(2.11)	0.70	(0.34)	0.71	(4.74)	(8.5%)
Brown & Sharpe	(0.23)	2.18	1.32	(0.26)	(0.25)	0.72	n/a
Cinc.–Milacron	(0.46)	0.80	(1.92)	0.98	(3.35)	1.02	n/a
Cross & Trecker	0.30	0.33	0.95	0.02	(1.62)	(1.82)	n/a
Gleason	(0.73)	(0.18)	(0.14)	0.06	(0.74)	(0.74)	0.3%
Dividends/Share ($mm)							
Loeffler	–	–	–	–	–	–	–
Acme–Clev.	0.90	0.40	0.40	0.40	0.40	0.40	(15.0%)
Brown & Sharpe	0.15	0.15	0.15	0.30	0.30	0.31	15.6%
Cinc.–Milacron	0.72	0.72	0.72	0.72	0.72	0.72	0.0%
Cross & Trecker	0.80	0.80	0.80	0.60	–	–	n/a
Gleason	–	–	–	–	–	–	n/a

Part VI
Working Capital Management

Case 17
Flanihan Engineering and Construction, Inc.

Although he had been on the job for only a few weeks, Raymond Meyer knew that the company's working capital situation would not wait for his education and indoctrination to the construction services industry. Having spent the past 20–some years in a manufacturing environment, he knew that he would have to rely on his assistant, Janet St. Clair, Flanihan Engineering and Construction's treasurer, for basic knowledge of the company's operations and, he hoped, a little insight into the nuances of trade receivables and payables.

As the firm's new CFO, he had devoted most of his time since arriving to studying the financial statements (EXHIBITS 1 and 2). From what he could see, he probably had a relatively urgent $10–$15 million working capital problem. But more importantly, the lack of a strict working capital policy would render whatever solution he might come up with as nothing more than the temporary extinction of another quickly flaring grass fire. Given that, Mr. Meyer called Ms. St. Clair and asked her to begin assembling industry norms on working capital usage for study, as he devoted his immediate attention to accelerating the collection of the company's $50 million in receivables. The plan was to meet again in a few weeks, when he would have some time to concentrate on the on–going nature of this problem, and the industry experiences in relation to it.

The Company

To Ms. St. Clair's dismay, Flanihan Engineering and Construction was actually in three industries, not one, and the norms were quite different. Specifically, the company engages in Engineering Services (SIC 8711), Highway and Street Construction (SIC 1611), and Non–Residential Construction (SIC 1541). Over the last five years, revenues have been derived primarily from engineering (46 percent) and highway construction (37 percent), and to a lesser extent, commercial construction (17 percent). This does vary somewhat from year to year but has been fairly consistent over time.

The company began as a commercial contractor in the years following WWII, and grew rapidly over the next decade. It remained small, however, until its big break in the mid–1950s when it received a multi–million dollar bridge repair contract from the State of Ohio. By today's standards, this might seem like small change, but from that contract, and the equipment purchased to complete that agreement, Flanihan's developed its specialty in highway, bridge, and tunnel work, and has expanded into engineering and construction services for airports, railroads, and other transportation systems. A natural extension for the company's expertise was in sewer and water projects, and it now includes wastewater management, environmental services, solid and hazardous waste disposal, and geological services.

Sources: Data and information based on various publications, including S&P Stock Reports, RMA Annual Statement Studies.

By the nature of this business, the company relies heavily on government contracts, which account for over 60 percent of total revenues. Although there have been a few lean times in its half–century history, the federal, state, and local government business has been pretty dependable, and with progress billings, revenues are steady and predictable. Having said this, the company does fill in the gaps and business valleys with aggressive bidding on private commercial and industrial projects, and as such, enjoys steady earnings and a reputation for stable employment. With national policy now clearly focused on rebuilding infrastructure, and state and local governments also facing up to their years of neglect, companies like Flanihan's should prosper for many years to come.

One problem the company has to deal with periodically, though, is slow paying clients when the economy is weak. This is currently the most critical finance issue, but what really concerns Raymond Meyer is the way the company has responded to the problem, much more than the problem itself.

Working Capital Policy

About a week prior to their meeting, Mr. Meyer received the results of Ms. St. Clair's data collection efforts. The first page was a table of relevant financial ratios for Flanihan's (EXHIBIT 3) and the next three (EXHIBITS 4, 5, and 6), industry norms for the three principal industries in which the company is involved. The final page was a short, handwritten note indicating that she had spoken with the receivables and payables managers to familiarize herself with company practices in these areas, and was prepared to discuss the issues related to a formulation of working capital policy.

What Mr. Meyer was not aware of at this point was that Ms. St. Clair had been pushing for such a policy for more than a year with his predecessor, the retired 27–year veteran Mr. Zahn. It was all too apparent to Janet St. Clair in her role as treasurer that working capital management was everything to a company in the engineering services and construction industries.

Discussion Questions

1. What is a working capital policy? What issues does it address? What are the benefits of such a policy, both general and specific, for this firm?

2. From an analysis of just the company's own financial statements, what seem to be the problems with working capital?

3. Without any consideration for possible synergies of three different industry activities in which the company is involved, develop composite estimates of accounts receivables and payables for each of the five years for which norms are provided. How do these compare to actual balances? How do the resulting composite ratios compare to Flanihan's actual ratios? What information, in addition to that gained by the previous statement analysis, do these "industry" norms provide?

4. How would you characterize Flanihan's working capital philosophy? Realistically, how much better could the company do in managing these balances, and what are the gains and risks of pursuing such a course?

5. Calculate breakeven sales for a more conservative, and then more aggressive, policy, in terms of return on assets.

6. If the resulting changes in sales from the more conservative and aggressive policies were something other than breakeven levels, how much would the EBIT margin have to change (how much could expenses decrease or increase) to break even? Illustrate these relationships so they can be used to guide policy decisions.

7. What additional information would be useful for this analysis?

Exhibit 1
Statements of Financial Condition
1987–1991

($mm) Year Ended December 31	1987	1988	1989	1990	1991
Assets					
Cash	0.7	0.5	4.3	2.4	0.5
Receivables	12.3	15.0	17.3	39.1	50.0
Inventory and Other	8.3	9.3	11.4	2.1	13.8
Total Current Assets	21.3	24.8	33.0	43.6	64.3
Long–Term Assets	11.6	11.9	13.1	15.3	26.4
TOTAL ASSETS	32.9	36.7	46.1	58.9	90.7
Liabilities and Equity					
Accounts Payable	4.7	6.2	6.1	9.0	28.1
Other Current Liabilities	8.1	9.5	9.2	14.8	20.8
Total Current Liabilities	12.8	15.7	15.3	23.8	48.9
Long–Term Debt	5.7	4.8	0.3	2.0	4.8
Other Long–Term Capital	3.7	3.9	3.8	1.6	0.9
Common Equity	10.7	12.3	26.7	31.5	36.1
Total Invested Capital	20.1	21.0	30.8	35.1	41.8
TOTAL LIABILITIES AND EQUITY	32.9	36.7	46.1	58.9	90.7

Exhibit 2
Statements of Operations
1987–1991

($mm) Year Ended December 31	1987	1988	1989	1990	1991
Revenues	79.1	87.4	102.0	127.0	202.9
– Operating Expenses	75.3	82.6	96.4	121.1	194.2
Operating Income	3.8	4.8	5.6	5.9	8.7
– Depreciation	1.2	1.3	1.6	1.5	3.2
EBIT	2.6	3.5	4.0	4.4	5.5
– Interest Expense	0.7	0.8	0.6	0.2	0.3
Earnings Before Taxes	1.9	2.7	3.4	4.2	5.2
+ Other Income	0.3	(0.1)	0.5	1.2	1.3
Net Before Taxes	2.2	2.6	3.9	5.4	6.5
– Income Taxes	0.9	1.1	1.6	2.4	3.0
NET INCOME	1.3	1.5	2.3	3.0	3.5
CAPITAL EXPENDITURES	1.2	1.6	2.3	1.0	3.1

Exhibit 3
Flanihan Engineering and Construction, Inc.
Working Capital Financial Ratios
1987–1991

	1987	1988	1989	1990	1991
Current Ratio	1.7	1.6	2.2	1.8	1.3
Sales/Receivables	6.4	5.8	5.9	3.2	4.1
Sales/Payables	16.8	14.1	16.7	14.1	7.2
Receivables/Payables	2.6	2.4	2.8	4.3	1.8
Sales/Net Working Capital	9.3	9.6	5.8	6.4	13.2
Receivables/Total Assets	.374	.409	.375	.664	.551
Current Assets/Total Assets	.647	.676	.716	.740	.709
Payables/Total Assets	.143	.169	.132	.153	.310
Current Liabilities/Total Assets	.389	.428	.332	.404	.539

Exhibit 4
Industry Financial Ratios
SIC 8711 – Engineering Services

		1987	1988	1989	1990	1991
Current Ratio	Hi –	2.6	2.5	2.4	2.6	2.5
	Med –	1.6	1.6	1.6	1.6	1.6
	Lo –	1.2	1.2	1.1	1.2	1.2
Sales/Receivables	Hi –	8.3	7.6	8.3	8.0	8.1
	Med –	5.0	5.3	5.1	5.1	5.1
	Lo –	3.7	3.8	3.7	3.7	3.7
Receivables/Payables	Hi –	6.8	6.7	7.1	6.8	7.3
	Med –	4.4	4.3	4.5	4.4	4.6
	Lo –	3.2	3.1	3.3	3.2	3.4
Sales/Net Working Capital		9.9	9.9	10.7	10.7	10.0
Receivables/Total Assets		.459	.471	.473	.484	.480
Current Assets/Total Assets		.672	.678	.670	.666	.665
Payables/Total Assets		.104	.110	.106	.110	.105
Current Liabilities/Total Assets		.433	.432	.440	.433	.425

Exhibit 5
Industry Financial Ratios
SIC 1611 – Highway Construction

		1987	1988	1989	1990	1991
Current Ratio	Hi –	2.1	2.5	2.1	2.0	2.3
	Med –	1.3	1.6	1.6	1.5	1.6
	Lo –	0.9	1.2	1.3	1.3	1.2
Sales/Receivables	Hi –	10.5	9.9	9.8	10.9	11.5
	Med –	6.9	6.6	6.5	7.1	7.4
	Lo –	5.0	5.0	4.7	5.1	5.2
Receivables/Payables	Hi –	3.1	2.8	3.2	3.1	3.6
	Med –	1.9	1.9	1.9	1.9	2.1
	Lo –	1.4	1.3	1.3	1.4	1.4
Sales/Net Working Capital		23.2	11.7	13.2	11.3	12.7
Receivables/Total Assets		.211	.330	.315	.232	.309
Current Assets/Total Assets		.446	.565	.573	.497	.552
Payables/Total Assets		.095	.156	.182	.139	.157
Current Liabilities/Total Assets		.345	.360	.349	.321	.353

Exhibit 6
Industry Financial Ratios
SIC 1541 – Non–Residential Construction

		1987	1988	1989	1990	1991
Current Ratio	Hi –	3.3	2.1	1.8	1.4	1.9
	Med –	1.7	1.6	1.4	1.3	1.5
	Lo –	1.0	1.2	1.2	1.2	1.2
Sales/Receivables	Hi –	10.5	10.2	9.8	9.8	10.5
	Med –	6.9	6.8	7.0	7.1	7.4
	Lo –	5.2	5.1	5.3	5.3	5.4
Receivables/Payables	Hi –	2.0	2.0	2.0	2.0	2.0
	Med –	1.4	1.4	1.4	1.4	1.4
	Lo –	1.1	1.1	1.1	1.1	1.1
Sales/Net Working Capital		10.0	12.7	15.3	19.2	13.4
Receivables/Total Assets		.304	.449	.496	.485	.458
Current Assets/Total Assets		.660	.758	.817	.820	.771
Payables/Total Assets		.162	.303	.386	.428	.322
Current Liabilities/Total Assets		.399	.494	.577	.624	.518

Case 18
O. L. Kimps, Inc.

At this level, performance reviews were supposed to be a perfunctory matter. As senior vice–president of finance, Michael Allman was unaccustomed to seeing "areas of concern" in his annual review. The timing was particularly puzzling since he had recently completed the third in a series of major acquisitions for the company over the past two years, allowing sales to grow by over 50 percent. He was aware of the need to shed some of the fixed assets that were deemed redundant as a result of the merged operations, but working capital? Then the comment his banker had made a couple of months ago about the size of the company's line of credit popped into his head. He reread his review. What was the "problem with working capital policy"? Before his meeting next week with George Owen, the company's CEO, he decided he'd better take the bull by the horns.

It's funny, he was expecting nothing but glowing comments in his review—and a handsome raise too!

The Company

O.L. Kimps, Inc., is an old–line publisher of books and periodicals in engineering and related fields. This core business owns hundreds of popular titles in the student and professional markets and publishes almost 100 journals, over half of which are society periodicals. Its dictionaries and reference books are industry standards.

While these products and markets remain its publishing base, in the last two to three years, Kimps has developed a number of new activities, including a mail–order book–selling business, the market for testing materials in a variety of engineering specialties, computer–assisted instruction programs, and a successful line of home improvement books, as a spin–off of its technical school materials. Although not a primary goal for the company, printing contracts for unaffiliated customers grew to over 175. These contracts are sometimes used to fill in the valleys of cyclical book sales.

Historically, most of these publications were under the Kimps name, but now with the acquisition of well–known publishing houses, separate and distinct editorial and marketing operations now exist for the emerging computer and European books/periodicals markets. In recent years the industry has developed in two important ways. The first is the explosion of non–print products, and the second is the consolidation of the publishing industry in Europe. While the company continues to proclaim that it is not interested in growth for growth's sake, the potential for a well–positioned firm such as Kimps seems almost limitless.

The company's sales are tied largely to the economy, which remains sluggish in spite of it being an election year. Its solid base of sales to libraries generally helps moderate these swings. And the near–term outlook for both U.S. and European sales is good, if not spectacular, and should allow the company to develop its products and markets in an orderly fashion.

Sources: Data and information based on various publications, including S&P Stock Reports, S&P Industry Surveys, RMA Annual Statement Studies.

The other primary contributor is post secondary education, but this too is weak at present. The company has products for the full spectrum of engineering and technical needs and should benefit from improvement in any of the sectors of these markets. Used book sales of college textbooks have soared in recent years, from less than 20 percent to now over one–third of total sales, but this is being countered with custom publishing by Kimps and several other forward–looking firms.

But even against these adverse market trends, the company is expecting to gain market share, and should post a 9.5 percent increase in 1992. The company's overall financial performance is given in EXHIBITS 1, 2, and 3, for the 1987–1991 period, along with industry norms in EXHIBIT 4.

The significance of the three recent acquisitions should be clearly noted. First, they represented large dollar amounts, both in terms of cost and in what they are, and will be, contributing to sales and earnings. Second, they were important strategic actions, in that they gave the company an immediate and substantial presence in markets believed to be hot growth areas. Third, the size and nature of these acquired operations have changed fundamentally how the company is run. This is neither good nor bad, just different. And finally, they offer significant potential for higher volume sales for many of the company's core titles, the key to profitability in this industry.

One additional dimension to the company's activities which may not be apparent in the data concerns the need, and the ability, to be an effective competitor. Because of the pace of consolidation in the industry, both in the U.S. and in Europe, competitors are fewer, but much larger. They are also much better financed. It remains to be seen how this will play itself out, but the company must position itself for this new era.

Working Capital

The working capital "problem," if there was one, had to be based on either the volatility of short–term sources and uses of cash, or the relative importance of current assets and liabilities. Since current assets as a proportion of total assets was relatively low and the current ratio seemed to be in line with industry norms, Mr. Allman decided to concentrate first on cash flows. This also would give him a handle on the line of credit issue.

As a basis for developing intra–year cash flows, Mr. Allman extracted a number of key items from the quarterly statements for the last two years. These are given in EXHIBIT 5. There was clearly volatility in these numbers. But what did it mean? In the past he had just assumed it was an operational issue—just the seasonal nature of the business. Was there a financial policy issue here?

At this point he was torn between diving into a monthly cash flow analysis and circling back to the issue of the relative importance of current assets and liabilities. The monthly analysis was beyond his legal pad capabilities, and since he was still not completely comfortable with his abilities using a computer spreadsheet, the choice was easy. He'd give the monthly analysis to Holly Russell, his assistant, and focus his efforts on working capital policy.

He called Ms. Russell and explained basically what he wanted. At this point it was O.K. if it was a little rough, he just wanted to get a sense of what was happening on a monthly basis. In particular, he wanted to see what 1992 would look like.

Seasonal Activity

Like most businesses, Kimps' operations exhibit a definite seasonal pattern. The monthly levels of sales are shown in EXHIBIT 6 for 1990 and 1991. Approximately 20 percent of revenues are cash sales, with the remainder distributed rather uniformly over the collection period. Payables are generally paid within the 10–day cash discount period. Tax obligations are due 60 days after incurred. Capital expenditures, of course, have occurred irregularly, but did not need to be considered at this stage. In fact, net inflows are expected for the next year or two.

What this more detailed cash flow analysis would show was obviously not known at this point, but the implications of not being prepared for his meeting next week were all too clear for Michael Allman.

Discussion Questions

1. What types of problems exist in working capital management? In other words, what should Mr. Allman be looking for?

2. From standard statement analysis, what are Kimps' strengths and weaknesses in current asset/liability management?

3. What do the cash flow analyses reveal? What are the reasons for these findings?

4. Are there financial policy issues that need to be addressed? What impact would they have?

5. How should seasonal cash deficits be financed? What are the alternatives?

6. What do you think is Mr. Allman's problem?

7. What additional information would be useful for the analysis?

Exhibit 1
O.L. Kimps, Inc.
Statement of Operations, 1987–1991

($ mm)	1987	1988	1989	1990	1991
Revenues	76.0	87.0	97.0	122.0	147.0
– Operating Expenses	68.6	81.4	90.1	111.9	134.5
Operating Income	7.4	5.6	6.9	10.1	12.5
– Depreciation	2.6	3.2	4.0	4.6	6.2
EBIT	4.8	2.4	2.9	5.5	6.4
– Interest Expense	0.1	0.3	0.4	1.1	2.4
Earnings Before Taxes	4.7	2.1	2.5	4.4	4.0
+ Other Income	0.8	0.4	0.9	1.6	0.9
Net Before Taxes	5.5	2.5	3.4	6.0	4.9
– Income Taxes	2.0	0.8	1.0	2.0	1.5
NET INCOME	3.5	1.7	2.4	4.0	3.4

Exhibit 2
O.L. Kimps, Inc.
Statement of Financial Position, 1987–1991

($ mm)	1987	1988	1989	1990	1991
Assets					
Cash	17.0	13.6	14.8	3.7	6.7
Other Current Assets	20.9	26.4	26.0	49.3	57.5
Total Current Assets	37.9	40.0	40.8	53.0	64.2
Long–Term Assets	21.1	23.1	23.5	45.9	49.1
TOTAL ASSETS	59.0	63.1	64.3	98.9	113.3
Liabilities and Equity					
Total Current Liabilities	25.9	28.3	28.7	41.3	46.4
Other Long–Term Liabilities	0.0	0.0	0.0	3.9	3.8
Long–Term Debt	0.0	0.0	0.0	6.1	12.3
Other Long–Term Capital	1.4	2.1	1.9	4.5	3.4
Common Equity	31.7	32.7	33.7	43.1	47.4
Total Invested Capital	33.1	34.8	35.6	53.7	63.1
TOTAL LIABILITIES AND EQUITY	59.0	63.1	64.3	98.9	113.3

Exhibit 3
O.L. Kimps, Inc.
Statement of Cash Flows, 1987–1991

	1987	1988	1989	1990	1991
Cash Flow from Operations ($mm)					
Net Income	3.5	1.7	2.4	4.0	3.4
+ Depreciation	2.6	3.2	4.0	4.6	6.2
Working Capital from Operation	6.1	4.9	6.4	8.6	9.6
+ Short–Term Sources	3.2	2.4	0.4	12.6	5.1
– Short–Term Uses	1.0	5.5	(0.4)	23.3	8.2
Cash Flow from Operations	8.3	1.8	7.2	(2.1)	6.5
Cash Flow from Long–Term Investment					
Long–Term (Gross) Assets	9.4	5.2	4.4	27.0	9.4
Cash Flow from Long–Term Investment	9.4	5.2	4.4	27.0	9.4
Cash Flow from Long–Term Financing					
Long–Term Liabilities	0.3	0.7	(0.2)	12.6	5.0
Common Stock less Dividends	(1.4)	(0.7)	(1.4)	5.4	0.9
Cash Flow from Financing	(1.1)	0.0	(1.6)	18.0	5.9
NET CASH FLOW	(2.2)	(3.4)	1.2	(11.1)	3.0

Exhibit 4
Industry Ratios, 1987–1991

	1987	1988	1989	1990	1991
Current Ratio	1.7	1.5	1.5	1.5	1.6
Sales/Receivables	6.2	6.4	6.0	6.6	7.4
Cost of Sales/Inventory	3.2	3.4	3.7	3.1	3.2
Cost of Sales/Payables	7.1	6.5	7.5	8.8	5.8
Sales/Net Working Capital	7.7	9.8	8.9	8.2	8.0
Debt/Equity	1.7	1.9	2.1	2.0	1.9
Sales/Total Assets	1.6	1.8	1.8	1.8	1.8
Pretax Profit Margin	4.5	3.7	4.0	4.4	3.7
Pretax ROA	6.6	7.0	5.6	7.8	5.9
Pretax ROE	20.3	22.2	16.9	23.4	19.3

Exhibit 5
Selected Financial Statement Items
Quarterly, 1990 and 1991

($mm)	1990				1991			
	Q1	Q2	Q3	Q4	Q1	Q2	Q3	Q4
Sales	26.5	28.8	31.6	35.1	32.6	34.5	37.0	42.9
Cost of Goods Sold	12.7	13.1	14.3	16.0	15.3	15.7	17.4	19.5
Operating Expenses	13.2	13.5	12.7	16.4	15.7	16.1	15.2	19.6
Depreciation	1.1	1.1	1.2	1.2	1.5	1.5	1.6	1.6
Income Taxes	(0.1)	0.4	1.2	0.5	(0.1)	0.2	0.8	0.6
Net Income	(0.3)	0.9	2.3	1.0	(0.1)	0.6	1.7	1.2
Total Assets	88.4	86.4	90.2	98.9	100.7	95.3	96.8	113.3
Accounts Receivable	26.5	26.8	29.6	35.2	28.9	29.6	31.2	35.2
Inventory	16.8	17.9	17.7	16.8	18.9	19.6	20.0	22.3
Accounts Payable	0.9	1.2	1.1	1.5	1.3	1.2	1.3	2.1
Notes Payable	5.4	1.0	0.8	5.6	7.5	0.2	0.2	7.4
Total Current Liabilities	32.3	26.8	28.5	41.3	38.2	34.5	33.8	46.4

Exhibit 6
Monthly Sales, 1990 and 1991

	Jan	Feb	Mar	Apr	May	Jun	Jul	Aug	Sep	Oct	Nov	Dec
1990	8.4	8.8	9.3	9.4	9.6	9.8	10.1	10.6	10.9	11.8	12.5	10.8
1991	10.4	10.9	11.3	11.4	11.5	11.6	11.8	12.3	12.9	13.8	15.4	13.7

Case 19
The Ware Company

Cash. If there were any word which chronicled the Ware Company's history, it was cash. Alexander Ware began the catalog in the late 1970s with a large cash inheritance. It struggled through the early 80s because of the recessions, in a desperate need of cash. It was in such a weakened state, it eventually had to declare bankruptcy, and languished for more than two years until William Gentry, corporate council at the time, came up with the cash to save the company, and the jobs of over 1,500 loyal employees and friends. Now the company has another cash problem—too much cash! Mr. Gentry would hardly let himself think this, but as he studied the financial statements about to be released (EXHIBITS 1 and 2), the cash "problem" seemed to jump right off the page.

Company Background

The Ware Company markets men's and women's professional dress and casual clothes through a catalog/mail order (actually, 80 percent of orders are made by telephone now) operation based in northern Kentucky. Initially, the company began a niche business in professional women's apparel, early on seeing the need for working women's quality, affordably priced business attire, and the potential for catalog shopping. From this success, it gradually added more and more men's clothing, and marketed the Christmas sweaters relentlessly until it had a stable clientele of male, as well as female, customers. The addition of casual clothes several years later was a natural, especially for the demographic makeup of its customer base. Other related lines followed, with mixed results. Most offerings are traditionally styled, both to appeal to a broader range of customers and to minimize the probability of getting stuck with quickly dated merchandise. The formula, although conservative, has worked pretty well over the years.

Ware is a publicly held firm, although Mr. Gentry personally owns 41 percent of the shares outstanding and the employees (ESOP), another 17 percent. The company first went public in 1987 and has generated about a 16 percent annual compounded rate of return for its owners up to this point (EXHIBIT 3). The accounting rates of return have been quite a bit higher, which can be attributed principally to healthy margins and good inventory control. These in turn are a function of good merchandising and strong vendor relationships. In its recent history, the particularly good, and bad, times have been linked directly to some facet of one of these factors, and thus management devotes the bulk of its time addressing these issues.

The company has a 300,000 sq. ft. state-of-the-art warehouse and distribution facility in Carollton, Kentucky, a small manufacturing facility in North Carolina, and 20,000 sq. ft. at their corporate offices in Indianapolis. Its "boiler shop" is second to none in the industry, with the very latest in communication and computer technology. And just recently, it set up a telephone order and distribution center in the U.K. In short, the company has invested heavily in fixed assets, especially in comparison to the industry (note fixed asset turnover in EXHIBIT 4 in particular).

Sources: Data and information based on various publications, including S&P Stock Reports, S&P Industry Surveys.

The legacies of cash shortages and bankruptcy are in the background of every decision in this company, a part of every policy. Most noticeable is the absence of debt. Emergency loans are quickly paid back and the small amount of long–term notes that were used to bring the company out of bankruptcy in the mid–1980s has now been fully retired. This conservatism, as noted earlier, extends to the product lines as well, with lost sales a continuing nemesis.

Lack of a Long–Term Plan

Finally, this "family" company has grown as its markets and internal capabilities have allowed. Only once did it acquire another firm, and only recently has it tested international opportunities. Neither were part of an overall strategy, they just happened. This comes back to the "cash problem." Although the company is decidedly not in favor of growth for growth's sake, sales are expected to increase by 10 percent to 11 percent this year, and over 15 percent for the couple of years beyond that. With the operational efficiencies realized the last two years a sure bet to continue, a dedicated work force eager to succeed, and a deep, savvy management team, the Ware Company should be a cash cow for years to come—but with no grandiose plans for what to do with it.

Maybe from his unique position in the firm, Mr. Gentry is just more aware of the potential supply of funds, and the relatively few future needs. From looking at the financial statements, however, what the company should do with all the cash seemed like an obvious question, and one that William Gentry knew he would have to answer soon.

The Necessity for Formal Planning

Mr. Gentry decided to put this question to his colleagues for their reaction. He was not a real believer in management theories, formal organization planning models, and the like, but maybe it would be interesting to hear how others saw the future. Also, whatever course of action was ultimately chosen, including even the "do nothing different" plan, he thought it would be helpful to try to document, in financial terms, what that path would look like.

To insure thoughtful and creative discussion, he decided first to have a pre–meeting discussion to allow his management team to prepare their thoughts. And second, to stimulate creativity, he would schedule a two–day event at a nearby resort. Although he was starting to get a little excited about the potential benefits of such a meeting, in the back of his mind, he couldn't help but wonder if this wasn't just blowing some of the company's cash.

Discussion Questions

1. Analyze the Ware Company's cash flows of the last several years. What observations and conclusions can you draw from this analysis?

2. One thing that is apparent in this industry is that seemingly minor merchandising miscues quickly become major inventory problems, which consume vast sums of cash. Given this, how much cash is really too much?

3. Project the cash that this company could produce over the next three years. As a minimum, how much cash does it need?

4. If a company finds itself with a "cash problem," what are possible uses of it? Be as specific as possible. Discuss the advantages and disadvantages of these to this particular company.

5. Focusing specifically on dividends, should the company raise its dividend, by how much, and what would be the effects of such action?

6. Outline a strategic financial management plan from these analyses and present it as a formally prepared plan.

7. What additional information would be useful for this analysis?

Exhibit 1
Statements of Financial Condition
1988–1993

($mm) Year Ended January 31	1988	1989	1990	1991	1992	1993
Assets						
Cash	28	32	8	27	1	23
Receivables and Other	5	5	6	7	7	6
Inventory	45	67	86	74	123	106
Total Current Assets	78	104	100	108	131	135
Long–Term Assets	29	47	67	77	75	74
TOTAL ASSETS	107	151	167	185	206	209
Liabilities and Equity						
Accounts Payable	23	31	20	38	28	37
Short–Term Debt	2	0	1	2	15	0
Accruals and Other	14	21	23	21	32	30
Total Current Liabilities	39	52	44	61	75	67
Long–Term Debt	9	7	5	3	2	0
Other Long–Term Capital	2	1	3	5	2	3
Common Equity	57	92	115	117	127	139
Total Invested Capital	68	100	123	125	131	142
TOTAL LIABILITIES AND EQUITY	107	151	167	185	206	209

Exhibit 2
Statements of Operations
1988–1993

($mm) Year Ended January 31	1988	1989	1990	1991	1992	1993
Revenues	336	456	545	604	683	734
– Cost of Goods Sold	195	269	316	361	395	433
Gross Margin	141	187	229	243	288	301
– Operating Expenses	100	132	177	211	231	237
Operating Income	41	55	52	32	57	64
– Depreciation	3	4	5	7	7	8
EBIT	38	51	47	25	50	56
– Interest Expense	1	1	1	1	2	1
Earnings Before Taxes	37	50	46	24	48	55
+ Other Income	1	2	1	1	0	(1)
Net Before Taxes	38	52	47	25	48	54
– Income Taxes	16	20	18	10	19	20
NET INCOME	22	32	29	15	29	34

Exhibit 3
Per Share and Market Data
1988–1993

	1988	1989	1990	1991	1992	1993
Earnings/Share	$1.11	$1.61	$1.45	$0.75	$1.53	$1.85
Dividends/Share	0.20	0.20	0.20	0.20	0.20	0.20
Book Value/Share	2.88	4.63	5.75	5.85	6.70	7.56
Price – High	30.255	30.875	35.750	21.000	30.500	37.875
– Low	12.125	17.500	19.000	8.875	13.375	23.000

Exhibit 4
Industry Financial Ratios
(1989–1993)

	1989	1990	1991	1992	1993
Current Ratio	1.4	1.6	1.5	1.6	–
COGS/Inventory	3.7	4.0	4.5	4.9	–
Sales/Fixed Assets	22.5	31.0	20.0	24.9	–
Sales/Assets	2.9	3.1	3.1	3.1	–
Total Debt/Assets	65.9%	59.1%	61.7%	61.7%	–
Long–Term Debt/Total Capital	26.9%	19.8%	23.7%	21.9%	–
Pretax Return on Sales	2.2%	3.8%	2.5%	3.3%	–
Pretax Return on Assets	5.6%	8.4%	7.1%	9.4%	–
Pretax Return on Equity	19.6%	27.3%	19.6%	24.9%	–

Case 20
Woods of New Hampshire, Inc.

Over its 25–year history, this modest New England mill has evolved from a simple logging operation to a full–line supplier of cedar lumber and millwork. It has also expanded to include designing and packaging complete home building kits from its many products. Of its $40 million in annual revenues, about three–fourths is provided by these home and sunroom kits, and the rest by dimension lumber and below grade and other scrap. The shift from lumber to home packages has boosted its profit margin significantly but now creates a drag from excess inventory of various components mismatched in proportion with requirements of specific kit orders. Large excesses are easily liquidated in sales of dimension lumber or millwork, but smaller overstocks simply sit in waiting, which when totaled, might add up to 10–15 percent of the $3.2 million held in inventory. Thus, the $2.5–$3.0 million in pretax income Woods of New Hampshire generates each year could be enhanced, perhaps significantly. Like many U.S. producers, inventory management for this company is big business, and it has captured the attention of John "Jack" Kinnaird, Woods' president, since returning from an executive seminar on the subject a couple of months ago.

Nature of the Business

The company manufacturers pre–cut cedar homes and sunrooms in a modern Lancaster, New Hampshire, facility year around. It has limited logging activities of its own now, but processes purchased timber at a saw mill and millwork site nearby. Mill products and schedules are tied to manufacturing needs, but material requirements planning is crude by today's standards.

Most home packages and all sunrooms use a cavity wall and post–and–beam construction, but the company also offers 4–inch by 8–inch cedar timber home kits, which sell well. Since acquiring its exclusive supplier of windows and doors about 15 years ago, all of the cedar and Douglas fir framed windows and doors for its packages are made internally. Outside sales of these products, as well as its manufactured oak and maple flooring, have not been good. From its New Hampshire headquarters, its home and sunroom packages are sold and shipped to dealers and directly to customers, nationally and internationally.

Although justifiably proud of its long–time record of producing a high quality product virtually 100 percent on–schedule, the whole notion of production lead time and its attendant costs (which was discussed at length in the seminar Jack Kinnaird attended) was a real eye opener. As a result, Jack sees a real opportunity here, through better inventory control, for cost reduction, quality improvement, and greater customer satisfaction. Such gains are only possible, though, if inventory management is fully integrated into the production process, and the processes themselves are completely reorganized. In doing so, Jack Kinnaird hopes to begin a new chapter in an on–going story of success for Woods of New Hampshire, Inc.

Sources: Data and information based on various publications, including S&P Stock Reports.

As a basis for gauging the impact of this initiative on the company's performance, growth potential, and possibly future financing plans, Mr. Kinnaird decided to pull together several key ratios from the financial statements for starters. These are shown in EXHIBIT 1.

Overview of the New Inventory Control System

Currently, the various components required for its packages are produced in batches, roughly in the amounts and on the schedules needed for the kits being manufactured, and then stockpiled throughout its spacious yard in predetermined locations, by type of component. But even with these large stocks, some components are in short supply when needed (with a stockout cost of 11 percent per unit), and a change in setup at its mill is necessary (with an average cost of changeover of $67,000). Variability in quality has been minimal though, because this has always been closely monitored, but this variability in the amounts needed of various components versus stocks on hand, while not excessive, has been significant.

In a nutshell, the new inventory control system will hold all work–in–progress inventory on the production floor, on pallet–type bases and in standard "kanban" containers, in exact quantities required for the kits being built and packaged. Different areas of the plant will be used for the production of different kits, in concert with the configuration of orders, with some common sub–systems assembled between the kit manufacturing areas in which they are used. Thus, just by knowing what components go into each of the various kits, their costs (all of which can be easily computerized), and a quick visual observation of the plant floor, the quantities and costs of inventory can be known almost instantly and accurately. The only (only?) trick in pulling this off is in scheduling component manufacturing work in its mill and millwork facilities to feed this system.

Quantifying the Production–Inventory Control System

While acknowledging that the company was going to take the plunge, it seemed prudent to Philip Graham, Woods' vice–president of production, to stage the implementation of this new system, beginning with the production of its popular "Weekender" sunroom addition. Though not in complete agreement on this point, Mr. Kinnaird was willing to use this product as a prototype for analysis and planning, prior to implementation.

The Weekender sells for $12,000–$18,000, depending on options, takes 13 person–weeks to produce, and like all the company's products, costs (COGS) approximately 70 percent of the sales price to make. This popular product represents about 20 percent of total revenues. And although not exact, its materials and method of manufacture are similar to the post–and–beam home packages, so investment decisions for this model should be projectable to the company as a whole, at least as an initial approximation.

Approximately 40 percent of cost of goods sold is material, and the remainder labor (primarily production labor at $11.70/hour). About half of the materials cost is dimension lumber. For the average $15,000 Weekender package, dimension lumber makes up 21,000 board feet (unit cost of $0.10), 1/2,000th of total annual usage of dimension lumber for the company. Conservatively estimated, the cost of carrying inventory is 25 percent, and the minimum lead time for ordering material from its mills is six days.

Mr. Graham also wanted an estimate of the variability in demand for dimension lumber, per period. This was developed from historical data, and is shown in EXHIBIT 2. With these data, he felt he could estimate some notion of optimal inventory, with which the inventory investment resulting from the new production–inventory system could be compared.

Discussion Questions

1. When a company "orders" from itself (requiring periodic setup changes) and for large quantities of similar materials, what benefits does an economic order quantity (EOQ) model have for inventory management? What are the limitations of EOQ?

2. Assuming for the moment constant demand, per period, what is the EOQ, average inventory investment, daily usage, and reorder point for the company's fairly standard dimension lumber?

3. Given the variability in demand, per period, of that estimated by the company for its dimension lumber, what is the appropriate size of safety stock? What is the resulting average investment in dimension lumber inventory, including safety stock?

4. Project the effect on the company's total inventory, if this case of dimension lumber is representative of the other inventory items.

5. What effect will this alternative investment in inventory have on the firm's profitability and growth? Assume the debt/equity ratio remains the same.

6. Pre–packaged home kits obviously involve various inventory items that are combined in certain predetermined proportions. How do materials requirements planning (MRP) and just–in–time (JIT) systems each address this problem of inventory management? What are their weaknesses? Can EOQ be integrated with these methods?

7. What additional information would be useful for this analysis?

Exhibit 1
Selected Financial Performance Ratios
1987–1991

	1987	1988	1989	1990	1991
Pretax Profit Margin*	8.5%	5.3%	4.8%	6.4%	7.5%
Total Asset Turnover	2.3	2.5	2.5	1.9	1.5
COGS/Inventory	13.1	13.8	15.2	11.4	9.4
Liabilities/Assets	50.9%	46.6%	45.6%	43.9%	39.0%
Payout Ratio	0.0	0.0	0.0	0.0	0.0

* Income tax rate is 40%.

Exhibit 2
Variability in Demand per Period
As a Percent of Average Demand

Demand per Period	Probability
0.50	.05
0.625	.05
0.75	.10
0.875	.15
1.00	.30
1.125	.15
1.25	.10
1.375	.05
1.50	.05